Single Sex Stories:
Tales of Unmarried Sexuality and Faith

by
Stephen W. Simpson

University
PROFESSORS PRESS
www.universityprofessorespress.com
Colorado Springs, CO

In this thoroughly engaging book, professor, clinical psychologist and humbly self-described "amateur theologian" Steve Simpson sets out to reconsider, rework, and re-envision a Christian view of unmarried sexuality that transcends the shame-based, guilt-inducing approach so common in Evangelical Christian circles. He makes the case for passion, love of the body, self-respect, mutual concern, and care for the community as central to a healthy approach, while still offering plainly his belief that intercourse belongs in marriage. He shares what the Bible, research, and psychological theory have to say about this topic, but mostly he tells stories. Real stories. Sensitive stories. Emotionally rich and humanly complicated stories. And he does so with an enviable blend of humor, honesty, elegance, and a non-nonsense approach that will draw you in and get you thinking. A wonderful book for teens and young adults of faith as well as their parents.

Jennifer Kunst, PhD,
Clinical Psychologist, Psychoanalyst, and author of the book, *Wisdom from the Couch: Knowing and Growing Yourself from the Inside Out*

Single Sex Stories is a labor of love to Christian singles. Deeply informed by theology and psychology it avoids legalism and easy answers. By telling stories (a la Irving Yalom), Simpson manages to reach the reader in emotionally and transformative ways. He reminds us that sex is not just about "me" but about "us," the Body of Christ. I know of nothing like it in the Christian literature. I wish I had this book when I was single and I will make sure to get it in the hands of Christian singles everywhere.

Brad D. Strawn, PhD
Evelyn and Frank Freed Professor for the Integration of Psychology and Theology, Fuller Seminary, Graduate School of Psychology. Author/Editor of *Christianity and Psychoanalysis: A New Conversation* and *The Physical Nature of Christian Life: Neuroscience, Psychology, and the Church*

Bombarded with mixed messages about our bodies, our behavior, and the Bible, it's no wonder we struggle in developing healthy attitudes about sex when we're single and on our own. Based on his experiences working as a skilled therapist with individuals and couples, Simpson offers valuable insights that expand beyond rigid thinking on sexual matters. As the reader ponders the perplexing situations of the characters in these personal stories, learning is happening as we let go of twisted thinking and let God lead in all areas of life including our sex life—all with a grateful heart.

Vivian Fransen, author of *The Straight Spouse: A Memoir*

Woven into Simpson's compelling stories (ones that many single Christians will find familiar), he artfully integrates psychological research, pop psychology tips, spiritual wisdom, and a healthy dose of humor. *Single Sex Stories* shines a light on an overlooked issue within the Christian community—the natural sexual desires of unmarried Christians. Through humor, biblical scholarship, psychological research, and his own personal experience, Simpson calls out the taboos and prejudices of singles sexuality while offering a revolutionary and refreshing solution. Simpson brings his considerable clinical experience, decades as an educator, and a personal story as a Christian trying to navigate his way through the labyrinth of sexual morality to bring us a compendium of sexual parables. If you're seeking a list of dos and don'ts, this isn't your book. If you're comfortable with living in the tension, read on. Simpson bridges the considerable gap between conservative Christian teachings and progressive psychological thought with a touch that is both lighthearted and poignant. His use of stories helps us humanize a host of ethical dilemmas that are much easier resolved in theory than in real life. As each chapter revealed yet another piece of profound wisdom served in a hilarious and uplifting package, I was left wondering why we Christians insist on making this sex thing so damn difficult.

Ryan Howes, PhD, ABPP
Board certified clinical psychologist who writes for *Psychology Today* and the *Psychotherapy Networker Magazine;* founder of National Psychotherapy Day, and therapist in private practice in Pasadena, CA.

Table of Contents

Foreword

Here's a pretty roundabout way to introduce a book of sex stories, with a spaceship story. It's kind of a true story (except the object-at-light-speed part).

You and I shake hands. You get on a spaceship and zoom away at the speed of light. Not doing anything special that day, I sit down to wait for you to come home. While you're gone I keep checking my watch. You do too. My watch is going *tick, tick, tick* (as watches do). Yours, however, is going *tick . . . [PAUSE] . . . tick . . . [PAUSE] . . . tick*. Time is moving slower for you. After a bit, you turn around and come home, surprised to find me stooped and wrinkled, a hundred years old. You however, look as young and fresh as when you left. It's a crazy new reality we live in. Time is relative to where we're standing when we experience it.

Not many of us really understand the physics behind relativity. However, the idea has crept into our popular consciousness. *"Dude. It's all relative."* Once *time* is relative to where we're standing, *truth* isn't far behind. My truth over here, and yours over there, can be different, and both true.

For several decades now, the nature of everything has been changing. Truth is less fixed and absolute than it used to be. It used to be true here *and* there, then *and* now. But when we weren't looking, quantum physics seeped into our collective narrative, and our concept of reality was upended. It's change of the highest order, inverting our most basic instincts about everything.

And while the nature of truth has been upending how we think, technology has upended how we live. It has changed the nature of work (less muscle, more thinking). It has made it possible for women to enter the marketplace. It has changed how we bear children and fundamentally altered traditional gender, sex, and marriage norms. Marriage and family norms that worked in the agrarian–industrial world, no longer do. They were designed for a world that no longer exists.

These seismic changes in truth, technology, economics, and society aren't going away. They mark a turn in history that isn't going to un-turn. It's a frightening pace of change. Many long for the stability of the good old days.

But we can't get to the good old days from here.

When truth changed, our instincts changed. Everything follows from there. Our instincts are unraveling social institutions at a startling pace. The way we govern, and educate, and do business, and family, and religion, are rapidly deconstructing. They have to. Old institutions were designed to work in the world that no longer exists.

Again, it's a traumatic process. We feel whipsawed. Old ways don't work, but we haven't yet figured out new ways. It's natural to cling to what feels solid, secure, and traditional.

As a Christian minister, the deconstruction of religious norms and institutions occupies my life. The way we used to practice religion has stopped working. People are voting with their feet. Those who remain are preoccupied trying to get back the glory days. It's scary. It's painful. It *feels* like our religion is dying. It *doesn't* feel like we're undergoing a historically inevitable process, stripping down the old, discerning and rebuilding the new.

We Christians did really well these last five hundred years. We adapted our message to work seamlessly in the *fixed-and-certain-truth* world. We adapted so well, we ended up on top of the Western-civilization heap. We were respected. We were honored. People considered us the guardians of absolute truth. When society needed important answers, it came to us.

We've become victims of our own success. History is demanding we adapt again, but it is difficult to let go of that golden age. We swing between shrill insistence on the old ways or retreating in defense. At the moment history is demanding arduous change, we are circling the wagons, doubling down on certitude, absolute truth, and the conviction that we have it.

It's an understandable response. Church (and religion in general) is by nature a conservative institution. Our role in society is to *conserve* the tried-and-true wisdom of the past. It's a helpful role. We act as ballast in the world, holding the ship steady through the storms of time. It's helpful . . . except when it's not.

Every so often our conservative instincts betray us. When history *demands* change, *resisting* change is a problem. Even when Divine movement calls for change, our instincts are to keep things the same. Like the Pharisees before us, our attachment to the old ways puts us at odds with the new.

***

Of all the things we church folk are certain about, we are "certain-est" about what we know about sex. If there's anything we are confident about, it's that God doesn't want us to have sex until we marry. And for good reason. For centuries our no-sex-until-marriage rule captured a great deal of wisdom about human sexuality. In both agrarian and industrial societies, it helped us organize our lives for sexual well-being.

But in our upended world, sex norms that once worked, no longer do. For example, as our economy shifts from physical to mental work, it takes longer for young people to get ready for society. Marrying later has become a social and economic necessity. Once, kids could be ready to make a living (and marry) by their late teens. Now the complexity of work requires extended preparation. In response, the average age of marriage for women has risen to twenty-eight, and men twenty-nine. The time from puberty to marriage has gone from four or five years, to *fifteen*.

Many churches have responded by ratcheting up our commitment to the old rule.

It's understandable. We love our kids. For thousands of years, the rule saved us from heartache. It's not easy to admit even to ourselves that the old rule isn't working. But the fifteen-year problem is driven by forces that aren't going away. It creates a biologically untenable situation. For the fifteen years our young people are at the height of their sexual hunger, our rule just says "no." Unsurprisingly, even committed church kids don't follow it.

Our instinct is to shore up the tradition. We encourage our kids to make purity vows. We give them rings and take them on retreats. We encourage our youth ministers to keep the rule on the front burner. Boiling it down, we either encourage our kids to marry earlier or wait longer. It's a rock and a hard place. We pit our kids against either economic or biological forces. They're not winning. Again, social and sexual patterns have been permanently upended. Norms that were helpful for thousands of years are no longer helpful.

And by doubling down, we unwittingly hurt our kids.

***

My own church asked me for help thinking through how to approach sexuality with our kids. I did a podcast project that is about to be published as a book.* In the introduction, under the heading "who is this book for," I described one group.

> *This book is also for those steeped in traditional sexual norms. You are my people. But we've been struggling. Devout, and deeply committed people are no longer waiting for sex until marriage. Most of us don't understand the social forces driving our abandonment of the old rule. Most of us just blame ourselves. Good, devout people labor under a heavy load of religious condemnation. We tell ourselves we have failed God, failed our religion, just failed. I hope this book will help you see how we got where we are, and to imagine a faithful way forward.*

When we put our kids in an untenable sexual position, we condemn them to condemnation.

Stephen's book moved me deeply. I've spent my life with the people in his stories, devoted Christians, doing their best to honor God and be faithful to the commandments. But the pain in these stories highlights the cost we exact from our kids when we put more energy into propping up the traditional rule than accessing our wisdom.

I can imagine a complementary book to Stephen's, painful stories of those who don't access religion's sexual wisdom at all. When our society abandoned the church's sex rule, it abandoned religious wisdom along with it. Our society's new rule, *"everybody screws everybody as long as nobody gets hurt,"* yeah, it's not going well either. We are into the third generation giving the new rule a go. Its legacy is heartache, brittle relational bonds, and children without access to one parent or the other.

The demand of this moment in history is different from the demand of most such moments. There is an enormous task set before us. We must first distinguish between religion's sexual *wisdom*, and religion's sexual *rule*. They are not the same. Our wisdom is a great gift for our children, for our society. It invites us to think through readiness, health, timing, and pacing in our sexual relationships. It opens the door to healthy sexual journeys. Our society is awash in crushing sexual pain, among religious and non-religious alike. Wisdom is wisdom, because it mitigates pain. Our wisdom is a gift we can give.

Our rule, on the other hand, just says "no."

---

*   *Rethinking Sex-Ed. The Wisdom of Religion . . . Without the Crazy* (on Amazon soon).

Sexually educating our young people is not as easy as teaching them the old ways. The job before our generation is to dig deeply enough into our wisdom to discern its essence and apply it in a fundamentally different world. We must strip tradition back far enough to understand its originating insights, and translate them into a fundamentally different social, economic, technological, and epistemological environment.

It's a daunting task. It's intimidating. What if we get it wrong? What if we betray the tradition by even trying? It would be tempting to shrink from the task and leave this reformation work for the next generation... if it weren't for the stories you will read in this book.

If we shrink from the historical task before us, we condemn another generation of our children to the pain Stephen shares in this book. We'll leave another generation to choose between a religious rule that doesn't work, and a no-rules rule that doesn't work any better.

Again, it's daunting. But read these stories. Read them and weep for our young people. And after you do, let's get to the work that history is demanding of us. Let's rework religion's ancient sexual wisdom for the new world we live in.

Dr. Doug Hammack
North Raleigh Community Church Downtown
April 2018

Doug is the author of *Rethinking our Story: Can We Be Christian in the Quantum Era?* Doug has more than 20 years of experience in spiritual formation and leading spiritual communities. His undergraduate degree in history is from the University of California, and his masters and doctorate degrees are both from Fuller Theological Seminary.

Introduction:
Stories and Secrets

I was trembling and so was she. We didn't expect this to happen, but neither of us showed any signs of stopping.

Ninety minutes earlier I had been squeezing the steering wheel in frustration as I navigated my way to Jenny's house amidst the blaring, treacherous quagmire that Bostonians call "traffic." With all those geniuses at MIT and Harvard, why had no one devised a civilized road system by now? I despaired of ever finding Jenny's house as the motorists of Boston introduced me to new and creative uses for profanity. It never entered my mind that Jenny and I might soon be wrapped around each other, rolling around on her bed.

Jenny and I shared a kiss on the last night of a "Christian Youth Congress" in Colorado when we were sixteen. We were now both freshmen in college. We hadn't seen each other since we met at camp, but we kept in touch by mail and a phone call two or three times a year. We never fostered fantasies of long-distance romance, despite that wistful adolescent kiss under a canopy of Rocky Mountain stars. I lived in the South; she lived in New England. The distance, not to mention other romantic prospects, kept us realistic. But our shared love for Christ and similar interests in movies and music kept the friendship alive.

When my friend Frank asked if I wanted to go home with him to Boston over spring break, my first thought was *"I love you, Frank, but can I wait to see if someone invites me to Florida?"* But my second thought was *"Jenny lives in Boston!"* That was all it took for me to go someplace colder than North Carolina for spring break.

On the Thursday night of spring break, Frank loaned me his car and said, "Good luck" with a wink before tossing me into the maelstrom of Boston traffic. Ninety harrowing minutes later, I got my bearings and found Jenny's house.

As the door opened, I began to apologize for being late, but the words stuck in my throat. Standing before me was not the Jenny I had known at camp. That person had been a girl, cute and willowy with a perpetual ponytail. The person greeting me at her door was a woman. She was beautiful, sexy despite her modest t-shirt and jeans.

It was my first visceral, primitive experience of sexual desire. It wasn't lust; I had no specific intentions or fantasies. My body and brain just had an involuntary reaction from being exposed to the woman in front of me.

"Hi," I managed.

Jenny broke into warm, welcoming smile and spread her arms. "I cannot believe that, after all these years, you are standing at my front door," she said and swallowed me in a hug.

That hug was the point of no return. Thousands upon thousands of words have been written about the perils of kissing, but hardly anyone frets about the effect of two young, hormonal Christians shoving their bodies together in an embrace.

"My parents are on a ski trip in Vermont," said Jenny. "I was with them but I came back early to see you."

"I'm glad you did," I said. The precarious situation presented by her parents being gone hadn't registered with me yet.

We talked and laughed like lifelong friends for about an hour. Then we started making out.

No, we did not have sex, not even any of the kinds some Christians don't think count as sex. But we did plenty of other things I had never done before. I felt sensations so overpowering and so wonderful that, for a little while, nothing and no one existed except for Jenny and me. My whole world was pleasure and excitement.

We made out for three hours before falling asleep on her bed. I woke up groggy and hungry because we had missed dinner. Jenny stirred beside me.

"You can spend the night if you want to," she said.

Of course, I wanted to. I wanted it more than anything in the world.

I called Frank and asked if it would be weird or cause trouble with his parents. He laughed and said, "I will just say you are crashing with another friend tonight. They don't have to know who it is. And it's not like I'm lying. Technically."

Jenny and I ordered pizza and cuddled on the couch. We watched television for a couple of hours, and then went back to her bedroom.

"I'll be right back," she said, and went to the bathroom. She returned dressed in flannel pajamas, but she might as well have been wearing lingerie. Every physiological meter in my body flew into the red zone.

"You know we can't have sex," I said.

She gave me a soft punch in the chest. "I know that! You didn't think I was trying to ... "

"No!" I said. "I think I was saying that more for me than you." It was true.

"I would have worn something other than pajamas if I meant to have my way with you, Mr. Simpson," she said, and we both laughed.

Jenny folded her arms, and the oversize sleeves of her pajamas flopped over her hands. "Just cuddling, kissing, and sleeping, okay?"

"Done," I said.

We kept to the cuddling and kissing, but I got no sleep whatsoever.

The next morning, we got bagels and coffee before saying goodbye. It was the last time I ever saw her.

Driving back to Frank's house, the thrill of being with Jenny gave way to another sensation. First, I felt nauseous. Next, sadness crept up from my stomach as my breath shortened. Then I had tears in my eyes.

"Oh, God," I began to pray. "What have I done? How could I have given into lust like that with someone I haven't seen in three years? I am so weak, Father. I am so, so sorry."

I felt like 165 pounds of sin. The shame swallowed me as I apologized over and over. I was convinced that I needed to repent, but I didn't know why or what for.

*****

Twenty-five years later, a nineteen-year-old girl sat in my psychotherapy office with tears in her eyes.

"We have only been dating a little more than a week, but I have been more physically intimate with him than anyone else."

I gave a slight nod to let her know she could keep going.

"I mean, we haven't had intercourse, but I've done things I never imagined doing before marriage. It's amazing at the time, and I don't even think about stopping, but the instant we aren't together anymore, I just feel so horrible."

"You feel ashamed?" I ventured.

"Yes!" she said through her tears.

Then I asked her the question that I wish someone had asked me after my night with Jenny.

"Why?"

She looked up, puzzled.

"Because . . . I don't know, it's wrong to put that much emphasis on physical intimacy."

"Okay," I said. "But how do you know that? This is obviously confusing for you, and we need to explore that. How do you know that you're doing something wrong?"

Her look of puzzlement turned into frustration.

"That's a good question," she said. "I guess that's just what I've always been taught."

*****

Did Jenny and I commit a sin? Did my client?

I am not saying that we didn't. I *am* saying that most Christians jump to conclusions based on assumptions when it comes to sexuality. Sometimes, maybe most of the time, those conclusions have little connection to the Bible or Christian doctrine. Psychological, cultural, and historical factors frequently mix up a cocktail of shame and confusion that gets mistaken for Christian faith. Sexuality is a lot more complicated than most of us have been led to believe. There is a lot more to it than questions of right or wrong, how far is too far, and when something is okay and when it is not okay. Sexuality as God created it cannot be reduced to a list of rules and regulations.

Like everything else that God created, sexuality is part of a story, one that begins at creation, culminates with the crucifixion and resurrection of Christ, and continues today in the Body of Christ and its members.

This is a book of stories about singles, sexuality, and faith. Most books about sexuality deal in theological and psychological principles. This one does, too, but our sexuality doesn't manifest in the ideological realm. It doesn't pop up in a seminar, at a church service, or during quiet moments of reflection with a self-help book. It's a visceral, sensory experience that hops into the middle of our life story. Sights, sounds, smells, and textures connect us with sexuality. The sound of someone's voice or the way hair falls around a face conjures a new feeling or an old one. A fragrance resurrects a memory long buried and forgotten. Hazy light passing through a window on a summer afternoon becomes forever linked to a powerful experience, whether we recall it with fondness or shame. Sexuality lives in our senses, in the scenes, sights, and sounds of life.

As a psychologist and an amateur theologian, I am a big fan of big ideas, but that's not where sexuality lives. Like everything else that matters, sexuality is part of our story. It would be easy to launch another book about the theology and psychology of sexuality into the world, but I think we have enough of those. If I share some stories about my clients and my friends instead, maybe you'll see some of your own story. Maybe you'll realize the power, importance, fragility, and sacredness of your own sexuality.

There's another reason I decided to tell stories instead of scribbling platitudes: Stories tell secrets. They let us into hidden places and reveal shrouded truths. The story of single sexuality in the Christian Church is the story of a secret. We hear cautionary tales that hint at the truth, but most are like ghost stories meant to scare children. The real story of sexuality is far more complicated. It's filled with sadness, but also joy. The true story has pain and injury, but also redemption and hope. It's time to tell the real story of sexuality for unmarried Christians.

We have to tell the truth, because the secrets and lies are corroding the Church. Secrets have power. They make us nervous and evasive. We burn up time and energy keeping them hidden. Some secrets — like a phobia of Tootsie Rolls or an obsession with Barbara Streisand's early work — aren't much trouble. But the big ones rule us. They jerk us around and tie us in knots as we go to ridiculous lengths to conceal them.

Most of us find mixing God and sex to be awkward at best, forbidden at worst. Some churches manage a seminar or retreat on sex once in a while, but even then it's discussed with great caution. Healthy discussions about single sexuality among Christians are rare. When we talk about sex at all, we usually stick to two subjects: marriage enrichment and sexual sin.

Marriage is the "get out of jail free" card for Christians when it comes to sex. It's as if there's an angel at a desk somewhere in heaven shouting, "We can stop watching Jane Smith, now! She just got married, so she can go as far as she wants without sinning!" We treat marriage as the brink past which sexual sin turns into "making love." That's great if you're on your honeymoon; it stinks if you're a single adult with hormones running amok. Our number one message about sexuality to unwed Christians is to "pretend it's not there until you're married."

Unless we're talking about sin. Then we talk about the emotional and spiritual damage premarital sex causes. We preach the perils of sexual temptation. We advocate pure thoughts and a pure bed until marriage. We teach men coping skills for staying away from dirty sites on the Internet, and we teach women to be modest with their bodies. I once attended a seminar led by Christian mental health professionals that devoted several minutes to teaching grown women how to sit properly so as not to appear immodest. We're good at letting each other and the world know how much trouble sexuality can bring. Though it's crucial to remember the consequences of sexuality apart from God's will, that's never been a problem for us. In fact, the Church went so far in emphasizing the depravity of sex that it inadvertently invented rock and roll.

In the 1930s and '40s, black gospel singers in the American South used the term "rocking" to describe spiritual rapture during a song. If someone was "rocking," they were filled with the Holy Spirit and having a blast in the name of the Lord (Tosches, 1991). Though we now associate "rocking" with head bobbing and fist pumping while the car stereo rattles the windshield, it was once a term of worship.

That changed in 1946, when blues singer Roy Brown wrote a song called "Good Rockin' Tonight." He never had success performing the song. Then, in 1951, a young man from Memphis named Elvis Presley recorded it. Cleveland disc jockey Alan Freed started playing the song on the radio along with other up-tempo rhythm and blues numbers. Freed coined the phrase "rock and roll" to describe this frenetic new music (Tosches, 1991). The rest, as they say, is history.

Though Christians were quick to label rock and roll the devil's music, Roy Brown began as a gospel singer. He borrowed the notion of "rocking" from his experiences in church. In "Good Rockin' Tonight," "rocking" is a double-entendre, using spiritual ecstasy as a metaphor for orgasm. Now here's my question: Why couldn't he have written the same song for church?

We all know the answer. You can't make that kind of comparison in church! It might even have offended you a little when you read it just now. But it's a good comparison. It makes sense that God would want the greatest expression of physical intimacy to approximate spiritual ecstasy. If drawing close to God is exhilarating, shouldn't we be comfortable comparing that to the experience that God created to bring man and woman physically closer than anything else? At some point, Christians got the idea that sexuality and spirituality don't mix. Maybe it was Plato, who told us that everything physical is imperfect and only ideas could be pure. Perhaps the Gnostics started it when they told first-century Christians that the body is depraved and corrupt. Maybe it was St. Augustine, who fretted endlessly about the trouble his sexuality caused him. Regardless, no one is singing songs about sex in church (Nelson, 1978).

The rest of Roy Brown's story is sad. He wrote rhythm and blues tunes for record companies that paid him little while making incredible profits off his songs. Only in the last year of his life did he finally enjoy the popularity he deserved (Tosches, 1991).

I wonder what would have happened if Roy Brown could have kept his music in church. What if he could have sung about the spiritual rapture of sex in the presence of his fellow Christians? Maybe he wouldn't have had to wander through nightclubs and juke joints trying to make a living. Maybe Christians would have revered his music, just as we revere The Song of Songs in Scripture. Maybe there'd be no such thing as Christian rock, because all rock and roll music would come from the Church's celebration of sexuality. What if rocking meant the same thing now as it did in the 1940's? I wonder if we missed a huge opportunity because we're too squeamish about mixing God and sex.

This book is about removing the power of secrecy from sexuality and embracing it as a gift from God. It's about helping single men and women feel whole and excited about their sexuality long before marriage and sexual intercourse. But married folks can read along, too. Whether you're married or single, there's a good chance your sexuality is a secret, severed from your sense of identity and your relationship with God.

First John 1: 5-7 says:

> This, in essence, is the message we heard from Christ and are passing on to you: God is light, pure light; there's not a trace of darkness in him. If we claim that we experience a shared life with him and continue to stumble around in the dark, we're obviously lying through our teeth—we're not living what we claim. But if we walk in the light, God himself being the light, we also experience a shared life with one another, as the sacrificed blood of Jesus, God's Son, purges all our sin. (The Message)

Single people have lingered too long in darkness. It's time for the Church to treat them like whole, indispensable members of the Body of Christ. We can start by hearing some of their stories.

The stories in this book are true but not real. They are inspired by real people and real events. The problems, the issues, the hopes, the fears, the grace, and the heroics are all true. In order to protect everyone's privacy, I put everything in a pot, swirled it around, and scooped out stories that look very different than the ones that really happened to my clients and friends. So the stories aren't real, but the things that happened are still true. More important, the stories are good.

Donald Miller, author of *Blue Like Jazz* (2003) and *A Million Miles in a Thousand Years* (2009), says that it's important to ask yourself whether or not you are living a good story. Would your story be one worth telling? Does it include suspense and risk and character growth? Is the goal worth the struggle, or is your story about living life on autopilot as you save up to buy a Volvo (one of Don's favorite examples)? The people I tell you about in this book decided to live good stories. They trusted God and ventured down Robert Frost's (1975) less traveled "road not taken." I think that's what matters most. Having good theology and the right beliefs is important. Teaching sound Biblical wisdom is essential. But these things must lead to living better stories, where faith and character defy the odds, where life pushes our trust in God to the limit and forces us to choose between redemption and despair. Don is right: Saving up for a Volvo isn't a good story.[†] But figuring out how to live as an unmarried Christian who can embrace and celebrate God's gift of sexuality without shame? Now that, my friend, is a great story.

[†] For the record, I drive a Volvo.

Chapter One:
Tara

Most people think that you measure a shrink's worth by the quality of their advice, but the real test of a therapist lies in what they *don't* say. A good psychotherapist excels at restraint. If I impose my opinions on a client without giving them a chance for deeper reflection, they won't figure things out on their own. If I tell them what to do all the time, they won't grow. I tell my students it's the difference between giving someone a flotation vest and teaching them to swim. I always share my thoughts sooner or later, but my main job is to provide a safe place for clients to sort things out. So I spend a lot of time holding my tongue.

Ten years after getting my license as a clinical psychologist, I fancied myself a pro at keeping my mouth shut when it mattered. I didn't know that I had yet to face my first real test.

Tara was a pretty typical referral for me. She was a single Christian in her mid-twenties, working in ministry. She was seeking therapy for "relationship struggles." Easy stuff, or so I thought.

I met Tara in the waiting room and invited her into my office. She was a midwestern Evangelical poster girl: Long dark hair pulled back into a playful ponytail, fair skin with just enough freckles, Carolina blue eyes, on the short side, lean but not too skinny. She wore a casual white top and trendy jeans. I don't know anything about women's shoes, but they looked like something other women might call "cute."

She sat up straight on the edge of my couch, all right angles. This was quite a feat considering that I'd intentionally bought a couch that swallows people, forcing them into a relaxed posture. We went through the informed consent paperwork and put it aside. I leaned back in my chair and said, "So, what brings you here?"

"It's a little embarrassing," she said. "My boss said I have to go to counseling or lose my job."

That sounded more complicated than "relationship struggles."

"Where do you work?" I asked.

"I'm the tour manager for a Christian artist. You've probably heard of her."

She told me the artist's name, provoking my first exercise in restraint. I had indeed heard of the artist. She was a Christian knock-off of Britney Spears, Miley Cyrus, Christina Aguilera, and a whole legion of ex-Mouseketeers. She could sing well enough, but the music was awful and the lyrics were worse. She sang songs of the "Jesus is my Boyfriend" ilk. Her latest album and tour were titled "Waiting for Him," an icky double entendre that meant saving sex for your husband while remaining a virgin in honor of Christ. I didn't like the play on words that mixed up Jesus with an earthly husband. I appreciated the sentiment and message, but the imagery and off-the-shelf pop music made me gag.

But the artist was popular, and who was I to say that God couldn't use syrupy garbage? Moreover, I had to put my feelings aside and focus on Tara.

Keeping my poker face, I said, "Yes, I've heard of her."

"Are you a fan?" Tara asked.

I don't impose my feelings on my clients, but I don't lie to them, either.

"Not really," I said.

"Good," she said. "I think that will help."

I remained silent, waiting for her to continue.

"I guess I'll just jump right in and get it over with. Like I said, I'm the tour manager. My boss is Doug, the artist's manager [let's call the artist Christina, just for fun]. Two weeks ago, I did something wrong. I felt terrible about it, so I confessed it to Doug. I really didn't know who else to tell, but he seemed like the authority in this situation."

I still didn't say anything but nodded to let her know I was listening. Tara was stalling, but I wasn't going to rush her.

"Anyway, I had sex with someone while we were on tour. It was someone I had just met, kind of a one-night stand."

Her face flushed and she looked down.

"I felt awful about it. And it's even worse because the theme of the tour is sexual purity. So I thought the best thing was to tell somebody."

"Christina's boss–"

"Doug."

"So Doug said you needed to get therapy?"

"Yes. And I got suspended without pay. I won't get my job back unless I successfully complete the disciplinary plan Doug gave me."

"What does this 'disciplinary plan' involve?"

"I have to go to therapy. I have to meet with Doug once a week. I have to meet with an accountability partner once a week. I'm not allowed to be alone with any male who isn't a family member. I also need to keep a journal of my devotional time and turn it in once a week. I have a curfew, and my mom or my college roommate has to send a text to Doug confirming that I'm home by 10 p.m. on weeknights and 11 p.m. on weekends. Doug was going to require me to go to a sexual addiction group, but Christina talked him out of it."

My fingers dug into the arm of my chair. This Doug guy was using a jackhammer on a thumbtack. Overreaction to sexual sin begins a shame cycle that only makes matters worse. All that Tara would learn from this is that she was broken and flawed. She would not experience grace or redemption. She would only learn that she was bad. If she didn't learn different soon, she would start to act that way.

Tara continued.

"I also had to make a public confession and apology to the whole touring crew."

My knuckles turned white. I hoped Tara didn't notice.

"Christina was really sweet about it. She pulled me aside and told me that she thought Doug was being too harsh and that she would talk to him about it."

Tara's head bowed, eyes fixed on the carpet. I took a breath and closed my eyes.

See the world from her eyes, not yours, I thought. *Do your job.*

I opened my eyes and exhaled, ready to begin.

"Okay," I said. "Let's start from the beginning."

*****

Tara and Christina had been singing together since second grade. They grew up in a church that kept an eye out for talent. It was one of those big nondenominational churches that met in a building that looked like a warehouse from the outside and a multimedia blitzkrieg from the inside. Tara and Christina started off in the children's choir, but Doug, the music minister, scooped them up to become backup singers in the worship band by the time they were eleven. It was adorable. Two cute little girls, one blonde, one brunette, punctuated the line of praise and worship singers. They lifted the Lord's name on high with pipes that belonged to a forty-year-old blues singer. Sometimes one of the girls would get a quick solo. Tara got the solos more often since her voice had a little more punch. If Christina was jealous, she never showed it.

Hours of practice and performance together made the girls best friends. They became inseparable. Despite Tara's chestnut hair and Christina's blonde hair, adults confused the two girls all the time. That changed when they turned fifteen.

When the girls hit adolescence, they both shot up a few inches and bonded further over blights of puberty. Then, between their freshman and sophomore years, Tara and Christina spent their first summer apart. Tara had been accepted to a summer fine arts program in New England for high school students. After wishing Christina a tearful farewell, Tara boarded a plane for Boston. She had the best summer of her life, studying music, creative writing, and drama. She returned to Los Angeles on Labor Day weekend, loaded with stories for her best friend.

She called Christina as soon as the plane landed. Christina was thrilled.

"Come over to my house as soon as you unpack," Christina insisted. "I'm hanging out by the pool, so bring your swimsuit."

"I can't wait!" squealed Tara.

Tara didn't stop smiling from the time the plane taxied up to the gate until her parents pulled into the driveway of her house. She was giddy until she unpacked and started to put on her . . . swimsuit.

Erg.

Three months spent indoors writing, playing piano, and working in a dim theater had left Tara with a complexion so pasty that it would embarrass a vampire. Her scholarly lifestyle, combined with Boston's culinary delights, had made her a little less lean. Tara didn't gain weight easily, but she had a little bit of New England chunk on her. No one else would notice . . . unless she put on a bathing suit.

She also hadn't updated her swimwear since she was thirteen or fourteen. She had a solid red one-piece, designed more for water sports than sunbathing.

You're being silly, she thought. *It's just Christina. Who cares?*

She put on her swimsuit under some shorts and a t-shirt and rushed to Christina's house.

Christina's mom opened the door and swallowed Tara in a hug.

"Everyone is out back by the pool," she said. "They are all so excited to see you!"

Everyone? thought Tara. *How many people are here?*

Tara walked around to the pool and found four people. All of them were male except for a girl in a bikini, lounging in a lawn chair with her eyes shut. She couldn't find Christina anywhere. She scanned the water and the patio. No Christina. Then her eyes went back to the girl in the bikini and she gasped.

She hadn't recognized Christina at first because she was unrecognizable. Her hair, dishwater blonde her whole life, was now a shiny platinum. But it was gorgeous, not tacky or fake looking. Christina's sun-darkened skin accentuated her hair and deep blue eyes. She was beautiful. But that's not what made Tara gasp.

When Tara left at the beginning of the summer, she and Christina were both gangly adolescents. They looked like "girls." Tara still looked the same, but Christina looked like a woman. Everybody had always said that Tara and Christina were both cute. In a mere three months, Christina had become something much more.

"Tara!"

Christina had spotted her. She jumped from her chair and pranced toward her across the wet concrete.

Get over yourself, Tara. Stop being so jealous and shallow. This is your best friend.

Christina hugged Tara.

"I have missed you so much!" Christina said, starting to cry.

That broke the spell and Tara smiled.

Then Christina said, "Where's your swimsuit?"

"Sorry," said Tara. "I forgot it."

*****

Two months later, Doug, the music minister, created a new musical group with Christina as lead vocalist. The amount of time and resources he invested suggested that this was a serious project. He handpicked the best young musicians from the congregation, young adults he had been grooming for over a decade. Christina insisted that Tara be in the band, so Doug made her a backup vocalist. Christina pointed out that Tara was also a skilled pianist, but Doug had already picked out a good-looking college guy to play keyboards. Christina bugged Doug about it until he agreed to put an electric piano in front of Tara and let her play an occasional second keyboard part.

Doug named the group "Manna" and started shopping it around all over Southern California as the perfect worship band for youth events. They were a novelty act—a bunch of talented kids, like The Jackson Five if they had been Christian, Caucasian, and much harder to dance to. But Tara knew Doug's true inspiration for forming the group was Christina.

Doug tapped Christina to be the lead vocalist for the same reason that Katy Perry, Beyonce, Taylor Swift, Rhianna, Britney Spears, Madonna, and a host of others before her had been chosen: She could sing *and* she was beautiful. Tara was happy for her friend. Really, she was. She loved Christina and could see that she was excited. But one of the hardest things for Tara to admit in therapy was that she was also crushed. Most people have a hard time admitting that two contradictory feelings can sit side by side in their hearts. Christians are terrible at it. They will ride a roller coaster of sadness, jealousy, anger, and all kinds of pain, all the while smiling and saying, "Praise the Lord!" Yes, Tara was happy for her friend. Yet, she was also devastated that a few physical changes made Christina seem more lovable. Tara knew this wasn't really the case, especially to God, but it still felt that way.

*****

Do a Google image search on the word "woman." Make sure you have the safety filters on, or you might get an eyeful of stuff you don't want. Did you notice any consistencies? Any themes? If your search turned up images similar to mine, almost all the pictures featured women who were lean, well dressed, well groomed, and attractive. Like Hollywood attractive.

Now do an image search for "Christian woman."

A little unsettling, isn't it? Other than scoring some points for ethnic diversity, those look like the same pretty, skinny ladies. I had to scroll past ten rows before I found a picture that looked anything like one of my old Sunday School teachers.

For all our talk about being "in the world and not of the world," the Church swallows worldly standards of beauty whole. This impacts men occasionally, but it affects women all the time. The Church objectifies women based on their appearance just as much as the world does. We're suckers for socially constructed notions of beauty, just like everyone else.

What we consider attractive, even sexually arousing, is socialized to some degree. Our culture tells us what is attractive, and our brains crystalize that information and link it to our reproductive drives. In Florence during the 1400s, pear-shaped women turned men on. If a modern supermodel went to Botticelli's studio looking for work, he would have shouted, "Get your bony behind out of here! I don't do paintings about the plague! Come back and see me after you've put on twenty or thirty pounds."

Christina took the leading role in the band because of her looks, and no one in the church had a problem with it. The message this sends to women and girls is "your appearance determines your value." The subtext of that message is "the more men want to have sex with you, the more valuable you are."

If the Church wants to be countercultural in promoting healthy sexuality, sex might not be the place to start. Maybe we need to start by being countercultural about beauty.

*****

After a few months, Tara learned to live in Christina's shadow. Performing with Manna, especially at different churches, was fun. She enjoyed playing music and even got to help with some of the arrangements. However, she became known as "Christina's friend" more and more. Guys were friendly with Tara as a means to meet Christina. Tara became chilly toward any new guy that was nice to her. She turned suspicious of longtime male friends if they started to call or text more than usual. Tara felt like a tiny planet orbiting Christina's bright star.

Tara might have quit the group and gone to a different church if Christina had not been militant about preserving their friendship. She texted Tara several times a day. She called Tara over the most minor life developments. She expressed unflagging interest in Tara's life. Had Christina expected Tara to become her number one fan, their friendship would have ended. If anything, Christina seemed more intent on focusing on Tara's life. Whenever conversations about Manna went on for more than a few minutes, Christina would say, "I don't want to talk about the band. Tell me what's going on with you." Christina acted like nothing had changed. That lasted until the True Love Waits event.

When Doug told the band that they had been invited to perform at True Love Waits, everyone in Manna knew that it was a turning point. True Love Waits was a massive youth event in Orange County. Christian bands would warm up the crowd for a handful of Christian speakers who would talk about the importance of sexual purity. At the end of the night, people would be invited to take an abstinence pledge. Over 10,000 people attended every year. It would be Manna's largest audience ever. Even Tara was excited.

The night of the performance, Doug called everyone together to pray before they went onstage. They took turns praying, as they usually did. When they were finished, Doug had an announcement.

"Last minute change, everyone," said Doug. "The program is ahead of schedule, so Christina is going to share a little bit of testimony tonight after the third song. It should take about 10 minutes or so. Everyone will just have to stand there I'm afraid, but I think it will be worth it."

Doug gave Christina a wink and she smiled.

Tara didn't know what to make of that. Christina sometimes talked between songs. She did a good job, but now she was about to give a mini-sermon. Tara tried hard to suppress the pinch of jealousy. Public speaking was one of Tara's strengths. She was chaplain of the youth group. She'd been performing in plays and musicals since she was ten years old. She gave speeches in front of the student council at school. Worst of all, she had coached Christina almost every time she had to speak in public. She had helped her work out what to say between songs. And now she was going to give ten-minute talk in front of 10,000 people?

Christina grabbed Tara's arm as they walked to the stage. "I just found out about this fifteen minutes ago, Tara," she said. "But this is actually something I've been thinking and praying about for a long time."

"What are you talking about?" said Tara, trying to act like nothing was wrong.

"You aren't upset?"

"About what?"

Christina stared at her for a moment and then sighed. "Good," she said. "Then pray for me. This is going to be intense."

Manna played their first three songs flawlessly. Christina sang her lungs out. The crowd ate it up. After the third song, Christina motioned for the crowd to be quiet. "It is such a blessing to be here! Thank you so much for having us. We're Manna, and my name is Christina. This event really has a special place in my heart because I really believe that true love does wait."

Cheers from the crowd.

"I want to share a little bit about why I've decided to wait. Sexual purity is one of the most important things in my life, and I intend to save one of God's most precious gifts and keep it locked away safe until my wedding night."

Manic applause and a few screams.

Tara's hand shot up to her mouth so she could suppress a laugh. She had never heard Christina talk like this before. She and Tara had talked about sex many times, especially on sleepovers. They were both committed to remaining virgins until marriage. But she'd never heard

Tara sound so . . . *holy* about it. Tara's voice even sounded weird. It was higher and she detected a hint of southern drawl. She ducked below her keyboard and pretended she was picking something up so she could release a burst of laughter.

"Do you mind if I share some of my testimony with you guys?" Tara asked the crowd. They howled in the affirmative.

When Christina finished a few minutes later, the audience roared so loud that the building shook. Tara saw people crying in the first few rows. Christina turned back to the band with her face aglow and cued the next song.

Tara had difficulty focusing on the music. She was stunned by what she had just witnessed and confused by her own feelings. Why did she feel anything less than total joy for Christina and the glory of the Lord?

Tara started to recover by the last song. Christina had gifts Tara didn't know about. That was a good thing. She asked God to forgive her for feeling anything other than happy. By the end of their concert, the happiness had taken over.

They left the stage embracing each other. Tara grabbed Christina in her arms and said, "I am so proud of you!"

Doug ran in, hugged Christina, and lifted her in the air.

After they vacated the stage, the next speaker came to the microphone. He was a man in his sixties. He had once been a big celebrity in Christian circles, famous for his videos about abstinence during the eighties. "Let's hear it for Manna!" he said and the crowd thundered in response.

"And how about that Christina?" he said. "Boy, let me tell you, if a girl that beautiful can pledge to save herself for marriage, everyone in this audience should be able to."

After hearing that, Tara excused herself. Everyone was too busy celebrating to notice her leave. Walking as fast as she could without running, she found a bathroom backstage. She stepped into a stall, knelt down, and vomited. Then she started to cry.

*****

After the True Love Waits show, it didn't take long for "Manna" to turn into "Christina." All of the interest from media and record labels focused on Christina and her purity message. Doug told the band it was an "unfortunate but necessary change" if they wanted to take things to "the next level and really glorify God."

Christina allowed the change on one condition: Everyone else stayed in the band and got a share of any royalties. Doug told her that this was unusual, but she wouldn't budge. As a result, Tara graduated high school with a part- time job that paid most of her college tuition at Biola University. She was a minor celebrity on campus because she was "in Christina's band." She was grateful for the life Christina had given her, even if she still resented living in her shadow.

Christina was attending college at Azusa Pacific, so Tara saw less of her than she ever had before. Christina still texted constantly and called two or three times a week. Still, Tara missed seeing her, especially outside of the band.

Then two things happened, almost without Tara noticing. First, other students at Biola stopped asking her questions about Christina. Boys who'd never heard of Christina flirted with her. Even better, some guys flirted with Tara *in spite* of her association with Christina. Christina's music had a distinct Top-40-meets-Praise-and-Worship style that college males rarely consider cool. Tara never would have admitted it, but she loved it when a young man extended an invitation to drop by his room and listen to some "real" music.

The other change was one that Tara's mother noticed first.

When Tara plowed into her house loaded with luggage at Christmas break, her mother's eyes went wide. "Oh my," she said. "You've become quite the woman."

"What do you mean?"

"The same thing happened to me in college. Some women just take a little longer to blossom. Your face, your hair, your body. They are all so beautiful. You've gone from being a pretty girl to a beautiful woman."

Tara flushed. "Um, thanks."

"We'll go bra shopping the day after Christmas."

Tara pretended like she didn't hear her mother and made a dash for the safety of her bedroom.

Tara's mom wasn't the only one who noticed something different.

The next time she saw Christina was at rehearsal for a Christmas concert at a big church in Porter Ranch. When Christina saw Tara, she couldn't stop gushing about how pretty she was.

"Sweetie, you have always been beautiful, but you have just really grown into yourself. And I love your clothes."

Tara had started to dress a little better. Her roommate at Biola was studying fashion design and couldn't keep her opinions to herself, so it had been inevitable.

When Doug saw her, he did a double-take. He stared at her for a moment, then seemed to shake it off. "Good to see you," he said, and then made small talk.

When they started rehearsal, Doug made a change to the stage set-up they'd maintained for over three years. Tara and her keyboard had always been on Christina's right, slightly behind her. Doug moved Tara to the back of the stage, next to the drum riser. She was almost invisible.

Then Doug saw to it that she became entirely invisible.

In April, the band began recording Christina's second album. The first album had been about chastity. The second album was about remaining pure for Christina's future husband, whoever he might be, and Jesus. So chastity again. Tara would have preferred a little variety, but she was getting paid to play music and tour the country with her best friend, so she tried to keep a good attitude.

Before the recording sessions began, Doug asked Tara to meet with him. She stopped by his office after church one Sunday. To her surprise, Christina was with him.

"Tara, we think it's time for you to take on a larger role in Christina's organization," said Doug.

Organization? Tara thought. *What does that mean?*

"You're great at what you do, but we think that your real gifts are in leadership."

Tara felt her muscles tense.

"Our tour this summer will be the biggest one ever. We need someone to be in charge of logistics, making sure the trains run on time. We need someone who can oversee the whole operation. At the same time, we also need someone who can be a spiritual leader and act as a chaplain. We're going to be on the road longer than we've ever been, and I think regular Bible studies are a must. I can only think of one person that has the gifts to do both of those jobs at once."

No, thought Tara. *NO!*

Christina, probably reading Tara's face, broke in.

"Tara, it would break my heart if you thought for a second that I didn't want you in the band."

Tara interrupted her. "Was this your idea?"

"No."

Good. She only had to hate Doug.

"But," Christina continued, "I really liked the idea after Doug explained it to me. I love having you on stage with me, but I'll be able to relax a lot more if I know that you're in charge of everything. You're a great singer — "

Better than you, bitch.

" — and a great musician. You'll be hard to replace. But I can't think of anyone else who could run the tour *and* keep everyone spiritually fed, including me. There's no one else I trust that much."

The guilt came in waves. She repented calling Christina such an awful word in her mind. God needed Tara to serve Christina. Maybe Tara could sing just as well. Maybe she could speak just as well or better. She was definitely just as much a virgin. But God had chosen Christina for the spotlight. God was using her voice and her beauty. Tara's role was to stay in the background and serve.

"Okay," said Tara, forcing a smile.

"You are the best," said Doug. "You just made me a happy man."

Christina let out a familiar squeal and clapped her hands.

Tara cocked an eyebrow and held up a hand. "Wait a second," she said. "I'm getting a raise, right?"

*****

Tara spent weeks learning about managing a touring production, reading anything she could get her hands on and interviewing any industry veteran that would talk to her. She memorized everything about every venue and visited some of the bigger ones in advance. She prepared weekly Bible studies. Aside from some expected glitches during the first two shows, Tara was masterful. Everyone got where they were supposed to be, when they were supposed to be there. They knew their jobs and did them. Every Sunday Tara lead a mini-worship service, featuring her own mini-sermon. She received nonstop praise from Christina and occasional compliments from Doug.

Tara should have been exhausted, but she had a reason to get out of bed every morning. It wasn't serving the Lord, though it should have been. It wasn't Christina, either. It was Tyler.

Tyler ran the lighting crew. Since a major lighting component was new to the show, Tara and Tyler spent a lot of time together. She had to learn about lighting from him, and he had to learn about the music and Christina's preferences from her. They developed a fun, easy rapport in a manner of days. He had a sharp wit and a playful personality. He was also handsome in a dark, rough-hewn way that was unusual for Christian boys.

It was Tara's first crush. She knew twenty-one was late for a first crush, but it didn't surprise her. Tara had never kissed a boy, though she didn't have any objection to it. She supported Christina's sexual purity message, but she had nothing against dating and romance. She just never thought of herself . . . like that. The notion that things like dating and kissing could be part of her life was new to her.

Christina's femininity and sexuality had always trumped Tara's acknowledgement of her own. Instead of becoming The Beauty, she became The Friend, The Helper, The Artist. The fact that her body had been vaguely androgynous through high school made it an easy choice. She inhabited her mind and spirit, but not her body. She was just waking up to the parts of herself that felt drawn to men. When she was with Tyler, she experienced new feelings, new sensations. They surprised her, but she enjoyed them.

Tara's anticipation grew as the tour crisscrossed the Midwest on its way toward Nashville. Doug had scheduled a four-day break following the show in Nashville. Nashville is Christian music's Mecca, so Christina would be doing a lot of media appearances and taking meetings with industry executives. This would leave the crew free to relax and frolic at the famous Gaylord Opryland Resort. Tara thought it was one of the most garish places in the world. The hotel's lobby was a massive atrium that smelled of chlorine. Beneath the glass dome was a landscape that asked guests to believe that two-story waterfalls, palm trees, Asian gardens, and a town from the antebellum South could all thrive under one roof. Tara hated it, but it provided plenty of places to play and lots of space to sneak away with someone. Someone like Tyler.

Tyler and Tara always went their separate ways after shows, so this would be their chance to spend some time together alone, away from work. She daydreamed about conversations beneath the tacky atrium that lasted until the wee hours of the morning. A first kiss wasn't on her list of objectives, but, if the moment arose, she wasn't about to stop it. Joshua Harris could go jump in a hole.

When they arrived at the hotel, Tara unpacked and took a long shower. She picked out her favorite clothes and was about to get dressed and go in search of Tyler. That's when she made the mistake of trying out the bed. This was her first real break in weeks, and the adrenaline keeping her on her feet called it quits. Her body felt heavy and slow all of a sudden. *Maybe I'll just close my eyes for a minute,* she thought. It was 4:00 p.m.

She woke up at 10:00 p.m. She jumped out of bed like she was late for work. She'd missed the whole evening! No, it was only 10 o'clock. Everyone on the crew was accustomed to late nights. Tyler and everyone else were probably wondering where she was. She told herself that her absence would only heighten his anticipation. She just had to find out where everyone was and make a grand entrance. She took a second shower to wash off her nap. Then she got dressed and whisked out the door.

She couldn't get reception on her phone until she was out of the elevator and in the hotel atrium. She walked out of the elevator and onto a long bridge crossing a fake lagoon. She was about to call Tyler when she noticed a couple about twenty yards ahead. They were holding hands and walking slowly. Tara started to tremble.

The couple stopped and turned toward each other. The dark-haired boy leaned down toward the girl with shiny blonde hair.

No, please don't. Please God make them stop.

Tyler gave Christina a gentle kiss on the lips. He pulled away, and Christina slipped a hand around his neck. Tyler kissed her a second time, and this kiss lasted forever.

Tara was still shaking, but she didn't cry. She couldn't. She felt numb. It was the same feeling she had when her father told her that her favorite aunt passed away. The same feeling she had when her beloved cocker spaniel, Freddie, had died. The tears always came, but only after the fog of unreality lifted. This time, Tara didn't want the fog to lift. She didn't want to feel anything. To her right, Tara saw a pink neon sign that said "Cantina" in an airy font that belonged in the eighties. She began drifting toward it.

The Cantina had something approaching a Mexican theme. A few people dotted the bar. A couple was at one of the tables. A few loud businessmen surrounded another. Tara shuffled toward the bar.

"What can I get you, young lady?" asked the bartender.

"A beer and a shot of tequila," she said.

Tara had heard people order that before when they were "partying." She'd never tasted tequila before, but now seemed like a good time.

"Can I see some ID?" asked the bartender.

Tara flipped upon her wallet to display her California driver's license.

"Twenty-one," said the bartender. "Just under the wire. What kind of beer do you want?"

"A Corona," she said because there was a neon sign advertising the beer behind the bar.

The bartender brought her the beer and the shot, which was larger than she expected. He also brought her salt and a lime for some reason.

Tara downed the tequila. It burned and she chased it right away with the beer.

"Whoa," said a male voice to her right. "I've never seen girl like you order something like that."

Tara looked and saw a guy whose picture probably popped up whenever someone did an online search for "hipster." Tight t-shirt with a funky logo, skinny jeans, low-cut Chucks. He had a stocking cap on his head, even though it was July.

"Yeah, so?" Tara said, almost snarling.

"Ouch," he said. "Don't take offense. Sorry. I'm just bored and trying to make conversation."

"It's okay," said Tara, not sure if she meant it. "I'm just not a big fan of men right now."

The hipster laughed. "We don't make it easy, do we?"

"No."

"I didn't mean to bug you. I'm just here with my band. We're trying to get signed, making the rounds. Hanging out with dudes all the time gets old. But I won't bug you anymore."

The hipster stopped talking. Tara looked at him from the corner of her eye. He was cute enough.

"In a band, huh?" she said.

"Yeah. We're kind of like an indie-blues thing."

"What's your name?"

The hipster smiled and stuck out his hand. "I'm Jeremy."

Tara took his hand. "I'm Tara."

"Nice to meet you, Tara. Can I buy you another drink?"

"Sure," she said. "Why not."

*****

Research shows that women who consider themselves unattractive are more willing to have sex than women who feel attractive. That's because most people buy into something sociologists call "sexual economics." If you want evidence that humans are fallen, sinful, and generally screwed-up, look no further than sexual economics.

Sexual economics states that sex has a "price," and women determine the price. A woman who feels attractive can demand more from a man before she offers him sex. Since her sense of value is intact, she can insist on things like a higher level of commitment, a more desirable mate, and greater compliance with her relationship demands.

A woman who feels unattractive won't "charge" as much for sex. Whether she's conscious of it or not, she will feel like she can't make as many demands from a man who displays interest. For example, she might not insist that they wait until they're married to have sex because she risks losing the man to a woman who is more attractive. Her only bargaining tool is to offer him more for his money (Regnerus, 2007)

If all this makes you want to vomit, congratulations; you have a soul.

But the research reveals a crucial catch in all this: If a woman *feels* attractive, regardless of how others rate her level of attractiveness, she will still demand a higher "price" for sex. And men will pay it.

Oh, and the opposite is true, as well. If other people think a woman is beautiful but she feels ugly, she will have a lower price for sex. Sometimes, a woman can feel unlovable because of past trauma or wounds from childhood, although people tell her she's pretty. She believes that sex is the only thing she has to offer in relationships.

The Christian approach to abstinence can be summed up in three words: "Don't do it!" Unless we start using a lot more words, this plays right into the hands of sexual economics. It says, "Sex has a price. Don't sell before you get marriage in return." If a woman feels attractive, her primary struggle will be managing her own sex drive and setting boundaries with any suitor who can't manage his.

Women who feel unattractive have it harder, facing a lose–lose situation. They often think, *If I don't have sex, I retain value by remaining pure, but I still feel undesirable. If I do have sex, it will make me feel like I have something of value to offer, but I won't be sexually pure.*

Sociologists discovered God's antidote to all this nonsense when they learned that a woman who *feels* attractive, regardless of what others think, has a sense of intrinsic value (Baumeister & Vohs, 2007). God intended us to love our bodies. That's why He created Adam and Eve in their birthday suits. If we feel beautiful, we'll act like it.

Maybe the abstinence movement should run with that. Instead of making people crazy by telling them "sex is bad" while simultaneously reinforcing the message that "sex is what gives you value," we can make sure that all women feel beautiful. We can teach them to love their bodies. We can teach girls that their value has nothing to do with putting a price on sex. They are valuable and lovable because that's how God makes people. He makes beauty in all shapes and sizes, and that's what's really beautiful. If we want to people to have healthy, holy sexuality, we should teach them their bodies are amazing. Feeling good about sexuality leads to the best decisions about sex.

*****

"So," said Tara. "That was him. That was the guy. One thing led to another, and I ended up back in his room. I didn't even really have to get that drunk. I'm not even sure why I did it. I guess I was just angry. Or curious. I don't know."

It was our fifth session. I had asked Tara to take her time telling me her story. I didn't want to miss anything.

"It sounds like you're not sure if you regret it," I said.

"I never thought of that, but I think you're right. I know it was a sin, but it also felt good to have someone just, I don't know, want me."

Some people think I can tell when someone's lying just because I'm a psychologist. That's not true. I'm sure people get away with lying to me all the time. But I can tell when things don't fit. Psychologists don't have magical powers of detection or persuasion, but we can tell if something doesn't make sense.

"So, let me get this straight," I said. "You had never kissed anyone before. We spent most of last session talking about how you don't understand how being a woman or a sexual person fits with your identity. You've spent the last few years of your life working for a musical artist whose message is sexual purity. From everything else I've picked up, you seem to have a lot of self-control, not to mention a strong sense of guilt. Despite all that, you got drunk and had sex with a stranger because you saw your best friend kiss a guy you had a crush on?"

Tara's brow furrowed and her eyes narrowed. If she wasn't angry with me, she was close. "What are you saying, Steve?"

"I'm saying that this doesn't make sense."

"I know! That's why I'm here. I'm trying to figure out why I did this."

"But you've already told me why. You said you were angry and you wanted to feel attractive."

That did it. Now she was mad. "Steve, don't take this the wrong way, but you're being kind of a jerk."

My most sociopathic clients rarely call me names, even when I deserve it. I was getting close to something that Tara was trying to protect. It was time to show her my cards.

"Tara, I don't think you had sex with anybody. I don't think you got drunk, and I don't think there was any hipster named Jeremy. I think you lied to Doug about it. And, you know what else? It makes perfect sense to me. It was a way for you to feel better about yourself and get away from Christina without hurting her."

Tara's face was frozen in outrage, but tears filled her eyes. After a moment, she looked down. Her hands went to her face and she started to cry.

"This is so humiliating," she said between sobs.

"I get that," I said. "But I also get why you did it."

"You're wrong about that part."

I love it when I'm wrong. It means I'm in for a surprise.

"Go on," I said.

"You're right about me lying, but I didn't do it just to get away from Christina. I didn't just do it because I was mad, either. It was because–"

Tara started bawling, hard. I was worried that she might hyperventilate. I told her to breathe into her stomach instead of her chest. After a couple minutes, she began to calm down.

"The reason I did it was so stupid," she said. "I just wanted people to think of me like . . . like someone that somebody would want to have sex with. Someone like Christina. I am so tired of being everyone's friend, everyone's damn nanny. But how could I do that, compared to Christina? I can't be prettier or more perfect or anything, The only way I could outdo her is to do the one thing everyone knows she won't do. That's the only way anyone might see me as . . ."

She trailed off.

"As what?"

"I don't know."

"Yes, you do."

"It's stupid."

"No, it's not."

"A woman!" she shouted.

Tears washed her face like a baptism. I sat with her in silence, in awe of her pain and her courage.

*****

I sometimes wonder what would have happened if a hipster named Jeremy really did hit on Tara that night. I wonder if she would have had sex with him. Regardless, I doubt it would have been hard for Tara to arrange some sort of tryst. It's not hard for a young woman to arrange a hook up in a hotel bar. She was willing to endure the public scorn for the sin, so why not commit the actual sin?

Maybe because sex wasn't the point; feeling sexual was. Despite the outrage that resulted from her fictional one-night stand, Tara was trying to show the world that she had just as much womanly value as Christina. She traded respect, community, and a good job for the chance to be thought of as more of a woman than Christina.

Tara bought into the lie we've all bought into: that a woman's worth is tied to her value as a sexual object. Telling another lie was only a small step.

Then, because God is good, and Tara is brave, she left the lies behind.

*****

Tara told Christina the truth. Christina told Doug right before she fired him. Christina was ready to start following her own vision as an artist, and that she couldn't do that with Doug as her manager.

Tara had her first kiss during her senior year of college. No beer, tequila, or hipsters were involved. She began dating a guy named Matthew, though it was hard to tell when they officially started dating because they had been friends for so long. They confessed deeper feelings for each other while listening to Van Morrison late on a Thursday evening. The following Sunday, Matthew kissed her when they were on top of Mt. Wilson at sunset.

We had our last session over three years after our first. There's a lot more to Tara's story. Tara discovered that none of this was Christina's fault. She uncovered deeper wounds, there long before Christina. Old hurts set her up to tolerate a system that made her feel like a machine instead of a woman. Over time, she developed a confidence rooted in her gifts — physical and spiritual — and the love of Christ. She feels like a woman in her own way, and she feels good about it. She feels at home in her own body, on her own terms.

Christina stopped being a yardstick by which Tara measured herself. As a result, their friendship became stronger than ever. Tara doesn't work for Christina anymore, and Christina wants Tara to record an album of her own. Tara's thinking about it, but she has mixed feelings. She's not eager to jump back into the Christian music scene. She's teaching high school English and drama now, but she's determined to go to graduate school for a Master's in fine arts.

At the end of our last session, it was hard to say goodbye. Tara had grown and suffered in my office, and seeing her once a week had become part of my life, too. I told her that it had been an honor for me to be a small part of her story.

On her way out the door she said, "I have a gift for you."

She handed me a flat square package. I could tell it was a CD.

"Open it," she said.

I pulled off the wrapping and saw Christina smiling up at me, her blonde hair blown by an unseen wind. Over her head was the title of the album, *Waiting for Him*.

I raised my eyebrows and shot a bemused look at Tara. Her face bore a wicked grin that I had never seen during our three years working together. I shook my head, and we both started laughing.

"I'm going to miss you, Steve," she said. "But Christina can keep you company."

I could have psychoanalyzed that to pieces, but I decided to let it go. We had talked about Christina enough.

Chapter Two:
Jonathan

That guy is way too chipper, and he flirts with no shame, I thought.

Jonathan was from San Diego, and he looked like it. He had green eyes and sandy blonde hair. He was tall and lean, but his broad shoulders kept him from looking lanky. He told everyone that he had never learned to surf, and that's probably the only reason I didn't hate him. Everything about him proclaimed, "I have come from the beach to take your women."

I wanted to charm the ladies at the retreat like Jonathan did, but dry wit and sarcasm were my social defaults as a college freshman (and, um, as a middle-aged man). This didn't click with the honeyed sincerity of the southern girls at Wake Forest's Intra-Greek Christian Fellowship Fall retreat. I was also the only college freshman in North Carolina with braces, so I kept smiling to a minimum. Meanwhile, Jonathan had the gleaming perma-grin of a mildly stoned saint. Maybe I really did hate him.

On the second day of the retreat, they organized us into same-sex small groups that would meet for the rest of the year. Guess who was in my group.

The first few meetings of our small group consisted of the facile "sharing" you get when a group of guys is faking vulnerability and authenticity. Everyone said the right things and provided the appropriate nods and humming noises. Jonathan specialized in "outside the box" thinking, championing the unpopular perspective by raising a point no one else had considered. I did my best not to vomit on him. The casual observer might have thought the group was getting closer, but we abandoned each other to our different fraternities outside of Bible study. If we saw each other on campus, we made quick Christian chit-chat and moved on. The small group and our real lives existed on separate planes.

The social structure at Wake Forest didn't help. The university has an unusually high percentage of three things: white people, nominal

Christians, and Greek letter organizations. This lack of diversity creates a breeding ground for cliques, the biggest of which are fraternities and sororities. Almost 60% of the student body at Wake joins a fraternity or sorority, compared to around 10% at most other schools. When two Wake Forest alums meet for the first time, there is an awkward pause before someone mutters "So, were you . . ." Then the other person will laugh and say which fraternity or sorority they were in. If one encounters a person who had the temerity to be "independent" in college, you congratulate them on their premature wisdom and then change the subject.

But Jonathan and I weren't just sheep in the Greek flock. We had been sheep in the Christian flock for much longer. That's how we ended up in Intra-Greek Christian Fellowship together.

A bunch of Christians at Wake Forest decided that Intra-Greek Christian Fellowship would be a way for Christians in different fraternities and sororities to make sure their brotherhood and sisterhood in Christ came before their brotherhood and sisterhood in Omega Kappa Banana Fo Fanna or whatever. It kind of worked sometimes. People made friends they wouldn't have otherwise. By Christmas time, however, I still wanted nothing to do with Jonathan.

I returned a day early from winter break because I wanted the campus to myself for a day. The tall trees, stately brick buildings, and vast lawns, unblemished by roaming herds of emerging adults, looked majestic and serene. An unsullied blanket of snow canvassed the ground, and silence was everywhere. I began to whisper Matsu Basho's poem "Winter Solitude" into the wind.

> Winter solitude
> in a world of one color
> the sound of –

"Dude!"

No other sound in the world could have ruined the moment so completely. I turned to see a tall guy wrapped from head to toe in ski gear. I knew who it was, though I could only see his eyes, those shining sea-green eyes.

"Hey, Jonathan," I sighed. "You're back early."

"Just like you! Did you think classes started today, too?"

"No," I said.

"Oh. Well, I'm glad you're here. Do you want to go sledding with me? I found an awesome hill on the other side of Reynolda Drive. We should be able to get plenty of speed and maybe a little air."

"Do you have a sled?" I asked.

"No, but I know how to sneak into the cafeteria. We can borrow a couple of trays. They're even better than a sled for this kind of snow."

I chuckled, forgetting the intrusion on my reverie. Sledding did sound like fun. My only hesitation came from the prospect of spending time with Jonathan.

"I don't know," I said. "It's getting late."

"Come on, man, you gotta go with me. I don't mind going alone, but it's more fun with someone else. Besides, I'm jonesing for another adrenaline rush after getting in some surfing over Christmas break."

"What?" I said. "I thought you didn't surf."

Jonathan's eyes popped wide within the hood of his red parka. Then he kicked some snow and made a grunting sound.

"What's wrong?" I asked.

Jonathan stared at the ground and didn't say anything for a few seconds.

"I don't want to be the dumb 'surfer dude,'" he said.

"Huh?"

"Come on, Steve. I know what you think of me. I know what everyone thinks of me. I can't help it. I grew up 200 yards from the beach. My parents surf. My big brother surfs. I was four years old when I got on the board for the first time. The way I look, the way I talk, the way I act, it's like something out of a bad surfer movie. People don't take me seriously. I thought I could at least get people to notice other things about me if I told them I didn't surf."

"Girls seem to like the whole surfer thing."

He grinned.

"Yeah, that's the one bonus. But most people assume I'm dumb, even the girls. Wake girls flirt with me but they won't date a guy they think is dumb. They never stick around to find out the truth. Like, what do you think my GPA is?"

No way I was falling for that.

"I don't know."

"Guess."

"Nope.

"4.0, dude."

At Wake Forest, meeting someone with 4.0 is like finding a four-leaf clover. When that someone is a frat boy who looks like Jonathan, it's like finding a four-leaf clover on an asteroid.

"You have a 4.0?" I said.

"Yeah," he said.

"And you're embarrassed about being a surfer?"

He sniffed. "Sounds stupid now that you put it that way."

I smiled and put a hand on his shoulder. "Show me how to sneak into the cafeteria so we can 'borrow' some trays and go sledding."

*****

Jonathan and I began talking to each other like real people instead of born-again actors auditioning for the next Kirk Cameron movie. We discovered that we liked the same music and movies. We had the same gripes about being in fraternities. We both lamented the fact that we didn't have the spine to be "independent" instead of Greek. But we had one thing in common that overshadowed everything else: We were both far more insecure than anyone knew. Insecurity for guys often comes from a weakness, like a bad habit or a characteristic others might find unattractive. For Jonathan and me, however, it was the past that haunted us.

The source of my low self-esteem wasn't complicated. As a child I had been overweight. As an adolescent, I developed a case of acne that made me look like I was in the first stage of turning into a zombie. By the time I reached college, I was lean and decent looking, but I didn't feel that way. You only had to scratch my veneer of snarky confidence for the shame to bleed out.

Jonathan's story was more complicated.

Jonathan had been diagnosed with dyslexia in the second grade. Dyslexia is a learning disability that makes your brain switch numbers and letters around. As soon as he was diagnosed, his school shipped him off to Special Education. However, as any psychologist with half a brain can tell you, having dyslexia doesn't mean that one is unintelligent. Fortunately, it didn't take long for Jonathan's Special Ed teacher to figure out that he didn't belong. She insisted that he return to his regular class and receive training outside of school for coping with dyslexia.

But the damage had been done. It would take years for the other children to let Jonathan forget that he'd done a tour of the Special Ed program. They nicknamed him "Special Eddie," which eventually became just "Eddie." Whenever Jonathan made a new friend, he would have to explain why everyone called him Eddie. Before long, the new friend would start calling him Eddie, too.

Jonathan made it his mission to overcome his nickname. He vowed to get excellent grades and get into a competitive college. To his surprise, the task proved an easy one. Beneath his learning disability and surfer-boy nonchalance lurked an intellect of ice and fire. Once he learned how to manage his dyslexia, his grades soared like a wave cresting off the shores of La Jolla.

But nobody cared. His teachers and parents lauded his success, but people kept calling him "Eddie" well into his freshman year of high school.

Then something happened that finally won the approval of the adolescent herd. Jonathan emerged from puberty looking like a genetic experiment that combined the DNA of A-list actors and half the male population of Sydney, Australia. All he had to do was flash a crooked smile and the ladies came running.

Jonathan was soon going on a lot of dates. Some of them were official dates, and sometimes he just got asked to "hang out" out at a cute girl's house with a bunch of her cute friends. His popularity spread across the gender divide, and guys started being nicer to him. He spent the summer between his freshman and sophomore year of high school surfing with new friends during the day and meeting girls at parties at night.

During the first week of sophomore year of high school, Jonathan was walking to class when a boxy, hairy guy named Alan walked into his path. Alan played offensive guard for the football team and had at least 50 pounds on Jonathan. Alan's second favorite sport behind football was taunting people who couldn't fight back, and Jonathan had long been one of his favorite victims.

"Hey, Special Eddie!" he shouted, turning heads up and down the hallway. "Welcome back! Did you finish learning the alphabet this summer? Are you going to be tying your own —"

A hand whooshed in from nowhere and smacked Alan in the back of the head. Jonathan heard the *thwack!* from ten feet away. The hand belonged to Cory Baker, the left side defensive tackle with twenty pounds on Alan. Alan looked at him in baffled protest.

"Baker! What the —"

"Shut up!" said Cory. "You had that coming. Make one more sound and you get another one."

Alan ducked into a nearby classroom, rubbing the back of his head. Cory Baker vanished without saying anything to Jonathan.

That was the last time anyone called him Special Eddie.

*****

By the end of our sophomore year, Jonathan and I didn't have to discuss whether or not we would be roommates during our junior year. It was a given. We bucked convention by living outside of our respective fraternity housing and sharing a room in an "independent" dorm. We got to be Greek and independent and best friends all at the same time. We were cheating the system and getting away with it.

We got more admiration than criticism. The brothers from Theta Chi gave me crap for moving out of the house, and the brothers of Sigma Chi did the same to Jonathan. The ladies on campus, however, thought we were rebels for putting friendship above our fraternities. Jonathan and I ate it up (neglecting to point out that real rebels wouldn't have joined a fraternity in the first place).

Our room became the social nexus for those eager to shuffle off "legalism," be it Christian or Greek. Jonathan and I had grown up in churches with a bad habit of observing the letter of the law over the spirit of the law and excluding people that didn't fit a particular Christian mold. During our first two years of college, we had learned that Christians were not the only ones who committed such sins. The secular world is full of organizations addicted to groupthink and threatened by outsiders, and Wake Forest had plenty of these. Academic departments, athletic teams, and even the allegedly countercultural college radio station where I was a DJ, all had their own dogma and criteria for membership. But fraternities and sororities were the worst. So Jonathan and I built loft beds in our room and created a mini-lounge for anyone and everyone who cared to join our little revolution.

The fall semester of our junior year was a season of perfection. When we needed to study or sleep, we shut the door and hung a "Do Not Disturb" sign boosted from a Best Western on the knob. At all other times, we welcomed Greeks and independents, Christians and Nons to hang out and play Spades, eat kettle chips, and engage in conversation serious or silly until the pre-dawn hours. We instituted a formal happy hour at four o'clock on Fridays to kick off the weekend. This was not some pedestrian keg party, oh no. Jonathan mixed martinis and Manhattans in a silver shaker for those old enough to drink legally and mature enough to drink responsibly. My job was to cook up a new mix tape at the radio station every week. The *piece de resistance* was a garish little disco ball Jonathan found at Walgreens. We hung it from the ceiling, and our happy patrons took turns using flashlights to shoot retro-dazzle dots of light all over the room. Every Friday afternoon, the population of our dorm room spilled out into the hall. The Resident Advisor might have complained if he hadn't been so busy "monitoring" the festivities.

A few weeks after the grand opening of Happy Hour, the energy in the room started to shift. The mass cacophony began to float apart into tiny bubbles consisting of one male and one female. These co-ed particles moved in patterns so predictable that it was like something out of chemistry class. First, a guy and a girl would pair up outside the room, leaning against a wall in the hallway and chatting. We called this "Stage One: The Hallway Approach." Next, they would end up sharing one of Jonathan's beverages together at our tiny bar, cobbled together from furniture scraps. This was "Stage Two: Beverage Flirtation." If that went well, they'd take a turn on our miniature dance floor, at first to one of my up-tempo selections, and then to one of the slow songs. This was known as "Stage Three: The Courtship Boogie." Finally, they would end up cuddled on a couch in the corner, also known as "Stage Four: PDR— Public Display of a Relationship." You could mark a couple's progress by their physical location during Happy Hour.

It made me so proud. Jonathan and I had provided a place for people to meet and fall in love outside of the fraternity party bacchanal. Dating was rare at Wake Forest. The culture didn't promote the integration of work and play. During the week, students were focused, serious, and interpersonally constipated. On Friday night, everyone would unsnap their scholarly girdles with some Jager shots and an evening around the keg. Cold stone inhibitions fell like dominoes. Girls who regarded me with all the warmth of a meter maid on Monday through Thursday would swallow me in long, suggestive hugs at first sight by 10 p.m. on Friday. On the weekends, two people who were friends (or less) would pair up in a dorm room to explore uncharted sexual territory.

Our Happy Hour was nothing like that. People met and started dating with the enthusiastic support of our little community. More than one marriage began with cuddling on the couch in the corner of our room. On Friday nights, our room was the place to blow off some steam without being stupid and get a little flirty without getting hurt.

I felt popular for the first time at college. I knew that I was riding Jonathan's coattails, but I didn't care. It was one of the best times of my life, and I saw no end in sight.

Then the ABC Club ruined everything.

*****

By the beginning of spring semester of junior year, I was in charge of mixing drinks for Happy Hour, in addition to mixing tapes. But I didn't mind, and neither did anyone else, even though Jonathan's drinks, even the non-alcoholic versions, were much better than mine. Everyone knew why Jonathan wasn't there, and everyone was happy for him. So was I, at first.

At the end of fall semester, Jonathan began Stage-One-Hallway-Approach maneuvers with a girl named Susan Rothschild. No big surprise, right? Jonathan is this good-looking guy who is throwing a weekly party at a campus that's safe and fun for everyone. He should have had women crawling all over him. And he did. But why was he still single well into his junior year?

Good question. In fact, you might wonder why I wasn't squared away with a lady of my own by this point. I was, but she was several hundred miles away. The summer after my freshman year, I went on a trip to Myrtle Beach with my high school buddies. While we were there, I met a girl named Meredith. We fell so hard and fast for each other that you'd have thought we were auditioning for the lead roles in *Grease*. Despite the fact that she lived in Maryland and went to Penn State, we resolved to make the relationship work. To the delight of AT&T stockholders everywhere, we were still hanging in there more than two years later.

The fact that I had a girlfriend made me an easy target for innocuous flirting during Happy Hour. The ladies of Wake Forest knew I had a girlfriend, and they knew I wouldn't cheat on her. Girls that would never touch me under different circumstances fastened themselves to my arm while I quivered like a hormonal hot water heater. Though Happy Hour was one of the best times of my life, certain moments almost made me black out.

Jonathan's love life was more of a mystery. He didn't have a girlfriend, but he would disappear with a new girl once or twice a semester. He would come home at dawn after "hanging out" with some attractive lady all night. Jonathan reassured me, with pride, that he was still a virgin and that he "never went too far," but he never revealed anything else. Jonathan and I talked about almost everything, including the never-ending drama of my long-distance relationship, but he was cryptic about his own love life. So the first thing that was so unusual about his relationship with Susan Rothschild was how open he was about it. Though I'd seen plenty of women catapult themselves at Jonathan, I'd never seen him pursue someone before. It was obvious that he liked Susan, and he didn't seem to mind people knowing.

The second unusual thing was that Susan was one of the few students at Wake Forest who wasn't even a nominal Christian. She'd come out as an atheist during freshman year by refusing to take part in any Wake Forest tradition with even a whiff of a religion. She never made a fuss about it, and she had plenty of Christian friends. But she refused to yield a single inch of her life to religion. If someone asked everyone to bow their heads in prayer, Susan Rothschild would slip her book bag over her shoulder and tiptoe toward the exit.

This soft defiance fit her image. She dressed in restrained alternative fashions, wearing ripped-just-enough-to-be-cool jeans and t-shirts with traditional punk iconography. She had pretty blonde hair and an expensive haircut with one modest streak of blue shooting down one side.

Jonathan and Susan made a perfect visual match. The handsome surfer and the pretty punkette looked adorable together whispering in the dark corners of our dorm room. Most people were excited when sparks started to fly between them, but I was worried.

The first night that Susan came to Happy Hour, Jonathan had spent almost three hours talking to her in the hallway. That night, he bent my ear until 3 a.m. about how "freaked out" he was because he might really like her. Before we drifted off to sleep I asked,

"What about the whole atheist thing? We both know that will be a problem."

"I trust God," he said.

"What does that mean?"

"I believe that God will guide me toward the right person. If it's Susan, then God will change her heart. If it's not, then things won't work out."

"Scripture reference, please."

"Shut up, Steve. You know what I mean."

I laughed.

"Just be careful," I said. "She's pretty hot."

"Yeah," said Jonathan. "She sure is."

By Thanksgiving, Jonathan was disappearing with Susan on a regular basis. They talked on the phone almost every day during Christmas break. By January, Jonathan and Susan would help me set up for Happy Hour, greet those first to arrive, and then vanish. By February, I only saw Jonathan early in the morning, late at night, and at our Intra-Greek Bible Study, when I could make it.

I missed Bible study for three weeks in a row in the middle of spring semester because of the NCAA Basketball Tournament. It's not that I was watching the tournament instead of coming to Bible study; it's that I was watching the tournament instead of doing anything related to Advanced Research Methods, Psychometric Theory, and Early Church History, three classes that were the scholarly equivalent of nightclub bouncers with short tempers. After the tournament was over, these classes hurled me into an alley and threw me an academic beat-down. I paid for my hours entranced by March Madness by spending all my free time running data analyses, reading about construct validity, and writing about Ignatius of Antioch and Irenaeus of Lyons. My extracurricular activities vanished, including Bible study.

When I returned to Bible study in April, everyone welcomed me back with minimal chastisement for my absence. The guys had been working through Matthew chapters five through seven, challenging each other to live out the commands of Christ. By the end, I felt refreshed and renewed. I'd forgotten how much I needed time with my friends and the Word of God.

When Bible study proper was finished, everyone hung around to talk, as always. The conversation following Bible study usually outlasted Bible study proper. We would talk about anything from sports to girls to school. One time a wrestling match broke out, and I had to pay for a lamp after becoming a little over-zealous. Anything could happen.

Ever since Jonathan and Susan started dating, women had become the most popular topic of post-Bible-study conversation. People talked about who they were seeing and who they had seen. They talked about first kisses with new girlfriends and bad break-ups with old ones. It was PG-rated locker room talk.

When I returned to Bible Study after my hiatus, something was different. The post-game conversation about the ladies had more of a smirk to it.

"Is Liz still making you keep the lights on when you guys make out?" Andy asked Mark.

"Yes," said Mark in an exasperated tone I had never heard from his holy "Young Life" mouth. "I can totally tell that she likes kissing and stuff, but she has this bizarre notion that turning out the lights will lead to sex. And I've told her I don't want to have sex before marriage!"

"Maybe it's not you she's worried about," said Andy. "Maybe she's afraid she'll get all hot bothered when the lights go out."

"Or maybe," said Jonathan. "She knows that she won't have to look at Mark's face when the lights are out, and then she might actually get turned on."

"Yeah," said Tim. "If she didn't have to look at you, she might even want to join the ABC Club."

"What's that?" I asked.

They all looked at me. Then they laughed.

"Steve," said Jonathan. "I haven't told you?"

"No, fartknocker. You don't really live in my room anymore, so when would you tell me?"

Jonathan ignored the dig. "'A-B-C stands for the 'Anything-But-Club.' It means anything but sex. The Bible says we can't have sex before marriage, but it's okay to do everything else. To get in the ABC club, you need to have gotten at least a hand job."

"Yeah, but–"

Andy cut me off.

"But a blow job is required for premium membership."

I was speechless, like someone was choking me. I looked at Mark. He smiled and said nothing.

"You guys don't think oral sex is the same as sex?" I asked.

"No!" said everyone but Mark.

"It doesn't say anything about it in the Bible. It just forbids sexual intercourse," said Tim.

I looked at Mark. "Is that true?" I already knew the answer, but Mark's opinion on this kind of thing mattered to me.

Mark shrugged. "Yes. Technically."

"Hey!" shouted Tim. "Who thinks Steve is in the ABC Club?"

"Hmmm," said Mark. "That's a good question." I couldn't believe that Mark didn't have a problem with this. Mark was the strongest Christian I had ever known, but this whole ABC Club thing didn't even make him flinch.

"I'm going to say yes," said Mark. "He's been dating Meredith for a while, and long-distance relationships make it a little easier. You have to stay under the same roof a lot more often."

"Nope, no way," said Andy. "Meredith doesn't seem like the type, and I've never seen Steve be anything but sarcastic around girls."

"I think it could go either way," said Tim. "But I'll bet Jonathan knows."

"Dude," I said, eyes wide at Jonathan, "Do not say a word."

Jonathan pantomimed zipping his mouth, locking it, and throwing away the key.

"So you guys are all in the ABC Club?" I asked.

"Everyone but Mark," said Jonathan. "But we think that's just because he can't close the deal with Liz."

I looked at Mark, who shrugged and said, "I'm still thinking about it and praying about it. The Bible is not clear. I know we all agree that you shouldn't get too intimate with someone unless you are in a serious relationship."

Nods of agreement all around.

"As for hand jobs, oral sex, orgasm, stuff like that, I'm still trying to figure it out. I'm praying about it."

In response to Mark's serious comments, a thoughtful silence subsumed the celebration of sexual legalism.

"But don't think I haven't done it because I can't close the deal," said Mark. "Believe me, if I wanted to join the ABC Club, I would be the president."

No one could trump that. Laughing, we all went home for the night.

*****

In 2005, the *Journal of Adolescent Health* reported the findings of a Yale–Columbia study examining at the sexual activity of more than 15,000 adolescents. It followed a group of teenagers who took an abstinence "pledge" or "promise" in the mid-1990s (Bersamin, Walker, Waiters, Fisher, & Grube, 2005). Most took the pledge as part of a program includes a detailed strategy for avoiding premarital sex. Pledgers can purchase special rings that say, things like "True Love Waits" in flowery script. The rings are often presented at a special ceremony. Some churches hold father–daughter banquets. The father walks his daughter up to the podium and places the abstinence ring on her finger. Over two million adolescents in the United States had taken the pledge at the time of the study.

Researchers compared the sexual behaviors of pledgers and non-pledgers (Bersamin et al., 2005).They followed both groups into their mid-twenties. Here's the good news: People who took the pledge waited an average of eighteen months longer to have sexual intercourse.

That does it for the good news.

As for the bad news, it's hard to know where to start. Eighty-eight percent (88%) of those who pledged not to have sex before marriage broke the pledge. But it's the things that pledgers did instead of having sexual intercourse that reveal the absolute failure of a prohibition-based approach to abstinence.

Pledgers were six times more likely than non-pledgers to have oral sex. They were four times more likely to have anal sex. Imagine the mental distortion that must take place for someone to consider anal sex less intimate than sexual intercourse. You only think like that if sexuality has become divorced from the self and God. When oral and anal sex are acceptable substitutes for sexual intercourse, sexuality has been reduced to rules and regulations. Intimacy becomes more about watching the speed limit than growing in life, love, and God.

The ABC Club was about getting as close to the line as possible without crossing it. It was about how much everyone could get away with. That's not what love and intimacy are about, much less a relationship with God.

Prevailing abstinence models treat sexuality like food that's bad for you but tastes really good. When it comes to consuming unhealthy fat in things like donuts and fries, health-conscious people ask, "How much can I have and still be healthy? Is it okay for me to eat this donut or these fries?"

The Bible treats sexuality like the healthy fat found in olive oil and fish oil. It asks, "How much of this do I need? How much is good for me?" The difference might seem subtle, but the distinction is important. With bad fats, most people want to indulge in the maximum amount that won't compromise their health. With good fats, you want to make sure you get enough to keep you healthy. When it comes to sexual behaviors, the question is rarely, "What is good for me? What blesses me and the other person?" Instead, it's "How much can I have before it's bad for me?" The assumption is that human sexuality and physical intimacy are fundamentally bad. Just like trans fat, you're better off without any (in this analogy, marriage is a fat-zapping miracle drug).

Behavioral restraint is important, and we still need sexual prohibitions. The Bible has plenty of them. The problem, however, is that people learn about the Biblical prohibitions as isolated verses instead of understanding them in context. If we look at the whole passage, we see that sexuality is not just about rules.

First Corinthians Chapter 6 provides an excellent example of how cherry-picking Bible verses leads to a myopic focus on prohibition over sexual wholeness. When someone wants to tell you how much trouble sexuality can cause, they frequently cite this chapter, which has no shortage of admonitions against sexual sin. What we often miss, however, is the logic Paul uses for his prohibitions. Paul's language reveals a powerful message about sexuality's role in our lives.

In verse thirteen, Paul compares sexuality to eating. Eating is fundamentally good. God created us to eat. It keeps us alive. Gluttony is a sin because it corrupts something that is fundamentally good. The message of 1 Corinthians Chapter 6 is that adultery, sex with prostitutes, and promiscuity corrupts the goodness of sexuality.

Paul goes beyond comparing our sexuality to food in verse fifteen:

> *Don't you realize that your bodies are actually parts of Christ? Should a man take his body, which is part of Christ, and join it to a prostitute? Never!* (New Living Translation)

Our bodies are part of Christ. Our *sexual* bodies are part of Christ. This is a radical departure from the Greco–Roman cultural norms the Corinthians knew and lived by. Paul needs to address Corinthian sexual behavior because Greek philosophy debased the body. They thought that the life of the mind was the only pure thing. The body was baggage, a useless and imperfect imitation of perfect heavenly forms. By this logic, it didn't really matter what you did with the body. The Corinthians would have been well acquainted with pagan sexual practices that Greeks regarded as nothing out of the ordinary. Having sex with a temple prostitute, for example, was commonplace, even for a married man in Greco–Roman culture. Paul makes it clear that our bodies are not a cumbersome shell for our souls. They are important, like food. They are part of Christ.

Evangelical attitudes about the body are much closer to Greek philosophy than Judeo–Christian tradition. Most Evangelical teachings about sexual purity regard the body as a thing to be managed, luggage to be dragged around until the resurrection. It's not an active, important part of our being, like eating. Paul's point is that sexuality is good, and that divorcing it from Christ leads to things like sleeping with prostitutes. This is not the prevailing sentiment when it comes to sexual purity.

Think about the last time you rationalized your way into a saturated-fat festival. Most of us can convince ourselves to eat something unhealthy if we conjure the right mental conditions. Here are a few examples:

> *It's the holidays. Everyone gains extra weight this time of year.*
> *I'll eat this now, but I won't eat breakfast tomorrow morning.*
> *This probably doesn't have that many calories.*
> *I'll exercise thirty extra minutes tomorrow.*
> *I shouldn't do this, but it tastes so good that I can't stop (even though I'll feel disgusted with myself later).*
> *Someone made this for me. It would be rude not to eat it.*
> *This is my favorite and I never get to have it. I can't miss the opportunity.*
> *I'm already fat anyway, so what's the point.*

We never think this way about healthy food. In fact, we probably don't think much of anything about healthy eating. We regard it as a fundamental part of life. But we have to do a few mental gymnastics before eating something we know isn't good for us. Unmarried Christians do the same thing with physical intimacy.

> *This is a special occasion. Maybe it's okay to go a little further this time.*
> *I'll do this now, but I'm living like a monk starting tomorrow.*
> *If I just put my hand down her pants; it's not as bad as sex.*
> *I'll spend some extra time in prayer and worship to make up for this.*
> *This feels so good I don't care if it's wrong (even though I'll feel disgusted with myself later).*
> *He/she really loves me. I don't want to make him/her feel rejected.*
> *Someone might never feel this way about me again. I can't blow this opportunity.*
> *I've already had sex, so what's the point of holding back?*

These excuses collapse under the slightest scrutiny, but people use them anyway. This is what happens when we split off sexuality from the rest of our being. Sexuality leaks out in momentary lapses of discipline. Sexuality becomes a mistake instead of part of our humanity.

*****

Between the end of spring finals and graduation at Wake Forest, fall three days with absolutely nothing scheduled. Students with the means and the permission decamp to Myrtle Beach, South Carolina. Students refer to this as "Post-Exams," but you could just as easily call it Beach Bacchanal, Excess Fest, Drunkapalooza, or Wake Forest Goes to Hell. William Blake once wrote, "You won't know what enough is until you know what too much is." Post-Exams is where people go to find out what too much is.

I didn't go, but Jonathan went and took Susan Rothschild with him. I remained behind to pack, planning to leave for home in Kentucky sometime the next day. I stayed up late trying to fit my sizable record collection (I hadn't transitioned to CDs yet) into a foot-locker. Around two a.m., the door burst open, and I spasmed in fright, sending my collection of Rush and Police albums flying across the room.

It was Jonathan. His face was red and he looked exhausted.

"What's the matter?" I asked. "Why aren't you at Post-Exams?"

"Is Mark still on campus?"

"No, he's back in Greensboro already."

"But that's only like thirty minutes away, right?" said Jonathan.

"Yeah, but it's two in the morning, man."

Jonathan paused, panting. "Okay," he said. "I think I can wait. I really need to talk to you and Mark, but I don't think I can tell this story twice. And I should probably sleep. I've been driving all day. I know this is weird, but can we go see Mark tomorrow and I can tell you what happened then?"

"Of course," I said.

"You don't mind heading back to Kentucky a little later?"

"No, it's fine. My parents won't care," I said, which was a lie. Mom made a big deal of homecomings, and this would ruin plans for a big meal or two. But Jonathan's panic told me this was would be worth the consequences.

Jonathan put a hand on my arm. "Thanks, man," he said, tears starting to roll down his cheeks. "You're the best."

We turned out the lights and got in our bunk beds. Before I shut my eyes, I said, "Is this about Susan?"

"Yes."

"How?"

"I'm sorry, Steve. I shouldn't have said anything. Can we just wait until tomorrow?"

"Okay," I said.

I tried to sleep but couldn't. I didn't drift off until the sky started to lighten outside. After no more than two hours of sleep, Jonathan shook me awake.

"We have to go. Now," he said.

I made him stop for coffee. Then he pulled onto the interstate and broke the speed limit all the way to Greensboro.

We arrived at Mark's house at lunchtime, shaky and sleep deprived. Mark's mom welcomed the hollow-eyed young men on her doorstep with a double dose of southern charm. She escorted us to the back porch. Mark reclined in a lawn chair reading John Piper or Tim Keller or Oswald Chambers or whatever daily fix he needed for his Reformed Theology addiction. He looked tan and relaxed, already in summer downtime mode. He had a summer job lined up at a Young Life camp in Canada, but he wouldn't be leaving for another three weeks.

"Welcome guys," he said. "Looks like school's not over yet, huh?"

"No," said Jonathan. "It's not."

We made small talk until Mark's mom finished putting out a spread of sandwiches, chips, cookies, and sweet iced tea. Then Jonathan began his story.

*****

"The more time I spent with Susan, the more I realized that the relationship wasn't going anywhere. We had fun hanging out and she's incredibly hot, but we just don't have enough in common. We don't see things the same way."

"Is it because she's an atheist?" I asked.

"That's part of it, but it's not just that. After we would get finished laughing and making out or whatever, we would just run out of things to talk about. It became obvious after a couple of months that marriage wasn't in our future. Well, it became obvious to me. Susan just seemed to be getting more serious."

Jonathan had decided that he was going to break up with Susan during Post-Exams. At a minimum, they were going to have to redefine the relationship and slow things down. He had planned to wait until the last day of Post-Exams so things wouldn't be awkward the whole time. He hadn't expected Susan to force his hand on the drive down to Myrtle Beach.

They had been riding along in silence for several minutes when Susan turned to him and said,

"I'm in love with you."

Jonathan didn't know what to say, but he didn't have to. The look of terror in his eyes told Susan everything.

"Oh no," she said. "I said it too soon, didn't I?"

"No. It's not that."

Jonathan confessed, as gently as he knew how, that he didn't see a future for their relationship. He assured her that this had nothing to do with how attractive or lovable she was. They were just too different, and he didn't see things lasting.

Susan rolled her lips behind her teeth and stared at the floor the car. She didn't say anything and Jonathan didn't push her to talk, even when the tears began. After a long, excruciating silence, she spoke.

"If you didn't see a future for us, then why the hell did you have sex with me?"

"What?" shouted Jonathan, his sensitivity vanishing.

"You shouldn't have sex with someone you don't love. I thought a nice Christian boy like you would know that."

"But we didn't have sex!"

"What? I went down on you! You went down on me! What did you think we were doing? Playing doctor?"

"That's not sexual intercourse, though."

"But it's still sex," said Susan. "How could you think me putting my mouth on your cock isn't just as intimate as sexual intercourse?"

"I . . . it's just not the same thing. Sexual intercourse is supposed to be saved for marriage and that other stuff isn't."

Susan's eyes narrowed.

"You are unbelievable. This is about you keeping your virginity, isn't it? You think you can do all that other stuff and still be a virgin as long as you don't screw somebody, is that it?"

"Well, yeah."

"You are such an asshole!"

"C'mon, Susan. Listen, I'm sorry. I never meant to– "

"Stop it! Don't say another word, you hypocritical bastard! You took advantage of me just so you could get off and still think that you are all holy and pure. I've got news for you Mr. Born Again Believer. We might as well have had sex. It's all the same to me."

"Susan, I had no idea. I'm so sorry."

"Take me back to campus."

"What? We're almost to the beach."

"Take me home or take me to the airport. Your choice."

Jonathan turned the car around and drove the four hours back to campus. Susan stared out the window with her arms crossed, refusing to speak to him. He pulled up in front of her dorm, got out of the car, and took her suitcase out of the trunk.

"Can I carry this up to your room for you?"

"No," she said, jerking the suitcase from his hand.

She began to walk away. Then she stopped and whirled around.

"One more thing, Jonathan. You are *not* a virgin. I don't care what anyone tells you. We had sex. Anything else you tell yourself is a lie."

And then she was gone.

*****

When Jonathan finished his story, we sat in silence for a minute or two. Jonathan's eyes were wet. Mark reclined in his lawn chair with a placid look on his face.

Finally, Jonathan said, "She's right, I guess. I'm not a virgin. It's a horrible thing to realize, but it's true. I've always been so proud of myself for remaining 'pure,' but I was just fooling myself. I feel so ashamed. I lost something I should have been saving for marriage, and I didn't even know it."

"That's not the point," said Mark.

Jonathan's head shot up, his teary eyes widening in surprise.

"What are you talking about? I'm not a virgin! I gave away something that I should have been saving for my wife!"

"That's true," said Mark. "I'm glad you know that now. I'm glad you shared that story with us, because I've been trying to work out what it means to be sexually pure myself. But the pain you're feeling is all about you. And, don't take this wrong way, man, but it's kind of an affront to God's grace."

"What?"

"Okay, so you're not a virgin. You committed a sin. Repent. Be reconciled to God. Wallowing in shame will only make this worse. God's grace is so much bigger than anything you've done wrong. If you act like this is some kind of permanent damage, then you're not trusting God's grace."

"Wow," said Jonathan, and nothing else. I didn't know what to say, either. Mark's words made sense intellectually, but they weren't connecting emotionally.

"Susan is the one you need to worry about. You sinned against her. You got too close too fast. The thing that really sucks is that she's not a believer. God will forgive you, but you made Christians look terrible. You hurt Susan, and you hurt the Church. I feel for you, dude, but I'm not really that worried about your sexual purity right now. That's the easy part."

Jonathan's tears stopped as stunned realization set in. It hit me, too. I knew that Mark was capable of prophet-grade insights, but this was a gut punch. A moment ago, I had been panicked over the fact that the rules for virginity had changed, but these new revelations hit me harder. God's grace was more than enough to repair the damage of sexual sin.

It wasn't about Jonathan. It was about what he did to Susan.

It wasn't about Jonathan or me or Mark. It was about the Body of Christ.

How could I have had it so wrong for so long?

*****

First Corinthians 6:19 says,

> *Don't you realize that your body is the temple of the Holy Spirit, who lives in you and was given to you by God? You do not belong to yourself.* (New Living Translation)

People often cite this verse as a call to sexual purity. If your body is a temple and the Holy Spirit lives inside, it makes sexual sin all the more appalling. It also makes it very personal, as if I sinned directly against the Holy Spirit.

Like everything in the New Testament, First Corinthians was written in Greek. Something important gets lost in the translation of this verse into English: The "you" is plural. *You* are not the temple of the Holy Spirit; *we* are.

A common mistake in Western culture is to think that Bible is talking to "me" instead of "us." The early church was far more "us" oriented than modern Evangelical culture. We like to think of the Bible as our personal owner's manual instead of bread for the Body of Christ.

Sex should indeed be saved for marriage, but not because it does irreparable harm to the individual. Regarding sexual sin as somehow permanent diminishes the power of God's grace. Though sexual sin, like all sin, can have personal consequences, chastity matters far more for the Body of Christ than the body of the individual.

We save sex for marriage so people understand that they are important and they are loved. They are made in the image of God, and this includes their bodies. The problem with premarital sex is not that it's dangerous to the individual; the problem is that it tells the world that the physical body is not worthy of great love. That's not what God had in mind. The Church has a responsibility to teach and show love. Our job is to make the world feel loved by God and loved by his Church. By valuing chastity before marriage, we show the world that we cherish love and intimacy. We don't decry premarital sex because it's such a terrible sin; we strive for chastity because we want people to love themselves as much as God does.

Sexual sins do not hurt the individual as much as they hurt the Church's ability to proclaim God's love for humanity. When someone looks at pornography, for example, the personal damage pales in comparison to the fact that they are using another person outside of the love of God. Yet, when someone comes to therapy for a pornography problem, they are almost always more concerned about their own spiritual and mental health than the women in the images they've seen. When we fixate on our own shame instead of our duty to show the world God's love, it's just another form of masturbation.

Jonathan's greatest transgression was not losing his virginity: It was failing to show Susan God's love. The consequences of his personal sin would be minimal. The damage to Susan, however, would be much harder to repair.

*****

Mark got up from his lawn chair and sat next to Jonathan. He put his arm around him and pulled him close.

"I feel so stupid," said Jonathan.

"I'm just figuring this stuff out, too," said Mark. " I don't know about you, but nobody in my church told me anything but 'Don't have sex!' It's a lot more complicated than we were led to believe. It's not like anyone gave us a road map for this kind of stuff. "

"I'm not sure that one exists," I said.

"It's a good thing we have a Guide, then," said Mark. "I just don't think we let Him lead us in this area very often. We grope around in the dark."

"Literally," said Jonathan. Mark laughed, easing the tension.

"So," said Mark. "I guess you have some work to do."

"I don't think Susan will want to talk to me for a long time."

"That doesn't let you off the hook."

Jonathan furrowed his brow and nodded.

"No. It doesn't."

I was quiet on the drive back to Winston-Salem. I felt dizzy. Over lunch with Jonathan and Mark, God had unleashed revelations that smashed long-solidified ideas about sexuality. Like Jonathan, part of my identity rested on these ideas. I didn't like what I had just learned.

When we got back to campus, I drove to the parking lot in front of Susan's dorm. Her car was still in the parking lot. Jonathan and I said a prayer. Then I instructed him to complete his mission or die of embarrassment in the effort.

I drove back to my dorm a little faster than I should have. I parked and bounded up the stairs two at a time until I reached my floor. I ran into the room, picked up the phone, and called Meredith.

She answered after the first ring.

"You sound out of breath," she said. "What's wrong?"

"Nothing" I said, "but I need to ask your forgiveness for some things."

Chapter Three:
Mia

"I didn't really want to have sex, but I got tired of saying no."

Mia didn't look sad as she told me about the first time she had sex at age sixteen. She didn't look anything. When someone tells me a heartbreaking story while their face shows no emotion, I get worried.

"That sounds awful," I said, as if reminding her.

She looked at me and smiled.

Showing no emotion is bad enough, but showing the opposite emotion is worse. Her brain had dialed up a defense mechanism that said, *I don't care if that shrink tells you it's awful; the feelings stay locked in the basement. You're showing nothing but smiles.*

Mia continued. "I guess after that, I felt like damaged goods. I mean, after you've lost your virginity, what's the point in not having sex?"

It was my turn to suppress emotion. I'd heard the "damaged goods" line too many times, and it always made me angry, though not at Mia. Mia didn't come up with the phrase "damaged goods." It comes from deep in a dark past, where the holy beauty of sexuality gave way to the lie that our bodies have a price tag.

*****

The waiting area for my office is on the first floor of the Graduate School of Psychology at Fuller Theological Seminary. Whenever Mia showed up, at least one male student ended up with whiplash from doing a double take. One time, a young man slammed himself right into the front door because he couldn't avert his eyes from Mia.

Mia couldn't remember a time when her beauty wasn't the only thing men cared about. Her parents told her she was pretty but taught her not to flaunt it. They raised her to be modest in her dress and manners. She learned to deflect complements with polite thanks and kind remarks in return. She was a delightful, modest, breathtaking Christian young lady.

She drove the boys at her church insane.

Mia grew up in a nondenominational megachurch in the San Fernando Valley. It was one those places with three Sunday services, greeters at every entrance, and a coffee shop on the campus. In such an environment, a gorgeous young woman with virtue and exceptional social skills triggers a feeding frenzy among Christian heterosexual males of breeding age. By the time she was twelve, men and boys lined up to offer everything from innocent compliments to lingering hugs. She learned early how to maneuver an embrace aiming for chest contact into a benign side-hug.

All these male overtures aggravated her father and worried her mother, but Mia thought it was fun. She had no interest in a boyfriend, but she liked being noticed.

That changed when she was fourteen. She started to notice boys almost as often as they noticed her. When they asked her on dates, she wanted to say yes sometimes. But her parents had forbidden her to date until she was sixteen. She argued with them to the point of tears and shouting, but they wouldn't budge.

Her parents' prohibition did nothing to stop the boys from asking. She turned away countless suitors, pushing against her own desires to reciprocate. By the time she was fifteen, she couldn't stand it anymore and started lying to her parents.

She didn't see it as lying at the time. She would tell her parents she was meeting "friends" at the mall or the movies. Technically, this would be true because she always went on double dates. If her parents asked who would be there, she would drop the name of a female friend and neglect to mention the presence of boys.

Mia's first few secret dates were innocent fun, filled with laughter and the thrill of clandestine activity. She held hands with her paramour, and if he earned a second date, she gave him a peck on the cheek as they said goodnight.

Then the boys began initiating plans to be alone with her. The two couples would go to someone's house, sans parents, and end up in separate rooms. Mia remembers being shocked by the sharp change in a boy's demeanor once he was alone with her. "He would change from a cute, cuddly puppy into a wolf!" she told me.

The boys from church weren't after sex, but they were after her body. She would consent to extended kissing sessions, but the relationship ended the instant a hand approached her breast.

"I only had to smack someone once," she said. "Christian boys aren't saints, but most of them can take no for an answer."

Disillusioned and discouraged, she fell back on her parents' counsel: no dating until she was sixteen. She thought she might even wait until she was eighteen so she could date men with more maturity and self-control.

Sexual purity was important to Mia in her early teens. Her church preached abstinence to the youth almost as much as they preached the gospel. Her youth leaders were emphatic about two things: First, she had to hold on to her virginity until marriage. Second, it was a gift from God that could only be given away once. The metaphors they used for virginity stayed with her for the rest of her life.

> *Your virginity is like a beautiful rose. Every time you have sex, a petal gets stripped away. Don't give your husband a bare stem.*
>
> *Your virginity should be a treasure locked in a safe, and only your husband has the key.*
>
> *Your virginity is a gift you give to your spouse on your wedding night.*
>
> *Your virginity is like a toothbrush. If a lot of people have had sex with you, it's like a lot of people have used the toothbrush.*
>
> *Your virginity is like a piece of gum. If someone takes it out of the wrapper and chews it, nobody else will want it.*

As Mia put it, "I learned that giving the gift away before marriage means you can never get it back. That made it worse than other sins, somehow."

*****

Evangelicals have a virginity fetish.

The Diagnostic and Statistical Manual of Mental Disorders, Fifth Edition (DSM-5) describes fetishism as sexual arousal by an inanimate object (American Psychiatric Association, 2013). While it's not fair to say that abstinence is sexually arousing to Evangelical Christians, it's pretty clear that we have a preoccupation with virginity as an inanimate object.

Let's examine some typical analogies for virginity: flower, treasure, gift, locked box, and even a toothbrush or a stick of gum.

My personal favorite turned up on an episode of "The Big Bang Theory." Sheldon and Leonard come home with brand new superhero action figures. Their friend Penny asks why they bought two of each action figure.

"One is to take out of the box and one is to leave in the box," says Leonard.

"Why would you want to leave one in the box?" asks Penny.

"Because if you take it out of the box it loses value!" says Sheldon.

Penny pauses. "I get it," she says. "My mom told me the same thing would happen to my virginity."

If any aspect of your sexuality is a thing instead of an integral part of your being, it can be tossed aside as easily as it can be locked away and treasured.

You might be thinking, "Come on, Steve, stop making such a big deal. These are just metaphors people use to teach kids to be careful. What's the problem?" The problem is that the words we use affect how we understand life. George Herbert Mead called this *symbolic interactionism* (Meltzer, Petras, & Reynolds, 1975) Metaphors and language form the basis for how we interpret life. The Christian symbolism for virginity commonly consists of inanimate objects like flowers, gifts, treasures, rings, and, apparently, chewing gum. By using this language, we make virginity a commodity. It's a thing distinct from your humanity.

When Christians refer to virginity as a "gift," they're comparing it to a gift-wrapped object, not a *spiritual* gift or a talent. It's a thing that you haul around until you get married, and then you give it to someone else. It never really belonged to you. I've read more than one Christian book on sex and marriage that say something like "your virginity/body/sex is not yours. It belongs to your spouse."

There are two huge problems with this logic: First, it implies that sexuality is never a gift for *you* and never part of who *you* are. God made sexuality a fundamental part of human beings. Disregarding it as irrelevant until you get married defies God's design. How much are you going to care about something that belongs to someone you've never met?

Second, implying that virginity is the only "gift" you need to save for marriage flings the doors wide open to a whole realm of physically intimate behaviors that don't qualify as sexual intercourse. Our churches are filled with "technical virgins," people who haven't had sexual intercourse but have done almost everything else, including behaviors that are just as intimate as sexual intercourse.

Theologian Martin Buber talked about the importance of having "I–Thou" relationships instead of "I–It" or "It–It" relationships (Buber,

1958). Recognizing yourself as an "I" means knowing and feeling the fullness of your humanity as created by God. Recognizing someone as a "Thou" means appreciating and acknowledging the same thing in them. If we see ourselves or someone else as an "It," we devalue the humanity and image of God.

Thanks to the Greeks, Romans, and their philosophical descendants, the modern Church treats sexuality like an "It." If you see part of yourself or someone else as an "It," you're not going to take good care of it, no matter how many times someone tells you to lock it up and hide it away.

*****

The boys with grabby hands convinced Mia to swear off dating. She planned to wait until college for her next dance with romance . . . until she met Justin.

Justin was a college freshman, not some frothing high school boy. She met him at a popular church camp in the San Bernardino mountains. He was part of the kitchen crew, but he didn't do dishes or bus tables. Justin could cook. He caught her eye on the first night as he announced the menu for the week before leading all the campers in the pre-dinner prayer.

She saw Justin again at the pool on one of his breaks. In addition to his culinary skills, the boy could do a bathing suit justice. Mia decided she wanted to meet him, and she knew exactly how to do it.

Justin and some other guys were taking turns seeing who could produce the biggest splash. Mia waited until it was his turn to jump in the water. Then she got up from her lounge chair and walked by the edge of the pool just as Justin leaped in. His splash drenched her and she squealed. She put her hands on her hips and waited until Justin's head popped out of the water.

"Nice work!" she shouted, feigning indignation. "I just spent ten minutes putting on sunscreen. Now I have to start all over!"

Then she stomped back to her chair. Justin shot out of the pool and trotted over to her. "I am so sorry," he said. "But didn't you see us jumping? I thought everyone could see we were making pretty huge splashes."

He has manners, but a brain and a spine, too, thought Mia. *Impressive.* She had gone too far to back down. "So you're saying this is my fault?"

"No, of course not," said Justin. "How about we say it was an accident. I didn't mean to splash you, but I'm still sorry. What can I do to make it up to you?"

"Well," she sighed. "I guess you could at least put some sunscreen on my back."

Five minutes later, they were joking and teasing each other.

That night after dinner, Justin bought Mia a milkshake at the snack bar. They talked past midnight, staying long after all the other chairs had been placed upside down on the tables.

For the next two nights, they held hands and took moonlit walks punctuated by gentle goodnight kisses. When they said goodbye at the end of camp, Mia knew it wasn't for good. Justin lived in Santa Clarita, only thirty minutes away from her. They already had plans for their first real date.

Mia fell hard and fast for Justin. He was smarter and funnier than anyone she had ever dated. He wasn't cute; he was handsome in an exotic way that made him more alluring than the boys her friends considered good-looking. She couldn't get enough of him. She spent every spare minute of the summer between her sophomore and junior year of high school with Justin.

As the weeks passed, they spent more time making out. She let him touch her. She liked it sometimes but didn't protest even when it made her uncomfortable. One Saturday afternoon, he started to unbutton her pants and she stopped him.

"What are you doing?" she asked. She said it playfully, not wanting to hurt his feelings.

"I want to be closer to you," he said.

"What does that mean, exactly?"

"I want to make love to you."

No, she thought. *I can't do that. That is the worst thing I could do.*

"I'm saving sex for marriage, babe," she said.

For the first time since she'd known him, Justin seemed irritated. "C'mon, I believe that, too," he said. "But I love you. I have never felt like this about anyone, and I know it's going to last. "

Mia gasped. It was the first time he had said he loved her. She put a hand on his face. "I love you too, Justin," she said, and kissed him. "But . . . This is a lot to take in right now. Can we at least take time to think and pray about it?"

Justin smiled and nodded. "You bet, babe."

That night, Mia thought and prayed. She fell asleep convinced that she and Justin should not have sex unless they got married.

The next time they made out, Justin started to unbutton her pants again, and she stopped him again. This time, he seemed angry. "You don't believe in us, do you?" he said.

"Of course, I do!"

"Do you love me?"

Now Mia was angry. "That's not fair. You know I do. And you better not think we need to have sex for me to prove it."

Justin put his hands over his face. "I'm sorry," he said. "It just gets kind of . . . painful down there for guys."

Mia giggled. "Yeah, I've heard about that. It's called 'blue balls,' right?"

"Blue balls, indeed," said Justin.

Mia stroked Justin's hair. "Well, maybe I can do something about it, at least," she said.

She had heard of "hand jobs" from girls at school but had no idea how to administer one. Suppressing a grimace, she improvised. It was messy, but it wasn't too bad. It was probably a sin, but it was better than losing her virginity. She hoped it would be enough for Justin.

It wasn't.

The next few times they made out, the hand job satiated Justin and kept him away from her pants. Then he went back to this business about being "closer" to her. He said a hand job was something she did for him, and he wanted them to share their bodies, but Mia didn't give in.

Justin and Mia planned a big date for Justin's final night before returning to college in Seattle. They had a romantic dinner and went to see a popular musical downtown. Justin spent a lot of money on great seats. Afterward, they walked beneath the fairy lights in the trees surrounding LA's Mark Taper Forum, savoring the summer benediction. It was perfect.

Justin took her back to the house he was renting for the summer with two other guys. His roommates were nowhere in sight. He took her by the hand and guided her up the bedroom. They always made out in his room after a date. Mia expected to set some boundaries with him, as usual, but she wasn't going to deny Justin physical affection on his last night before returning to college.

"I love you so much," he said.

"I love you, too," she said, and they started kissing.

When she guided Justin's hand away from her thigh, he stopped kissing her and sat up. He didn't seem frustrated this time. His eyes were intense as he looked at her for a long time without saying anything.

"You know we're going to get married someday," he said, at last.

Mia didn't know what to say. She loved the idea, but it seemed so far off. She was still in high school.

"That sounds really nice," she said.

"It's not just a nice idea; it's the truth," said Justin. "I want to make love to my future wife."

Looking back, Mia wonders if she was just tired. Tired because it was late. Tired of telling him no. Tired of telling herself no, because part of her wanted it, too. And she believed him, at least in that moment. She would be his wife one day. What was the point in resisting?

"All right," she said. "But you have to wear a condom."

"I've been saving one for just this moment," she said.

"Just promise me that's the only reason you have it," she said. "Promise me that I'm your first."

"I promise," he said.

Mia closed her eyes and took a deep breath.

"Okay," she said, and started to undress.

*****

Mia didn't sleep for the next three nights. She kicked at her sheets, rearranged her pillows, took Melatonin, drank chamomile, and even swiped an Ambien from her mother's medicine cabinet. Still, not a wink.

It was gone. The precious gift she had meant to save for marriage, that she was supposed to keep locked and hidden away, was gone. How could she have been so foolish? She felt sick, nauseated with grief over the loss. Her virginity had always been a crucial part of what made her feel like a Christian. Now that it was gone she wasn't sure who she was.

"I am so sorry God! Please forgive me!" These short, repetitive pleas for forgiveness were her only prayers. Otherwise, she was terrified to talk to God. She had given away one of his greatest gifts. How could He not hate her?

She tried to soothe the pain by texting Justin. At first, he responded right away with warmth and affection. When he started taking longer to answer, she would check her phone compulsively. Then she would call. When he didn't pick up, she didn't leave a voicemail. He could see that she had called, so surely he would get back to her soon.

In the two weeks after Justin left for college, he texted her only an agonizing thirteen times in response to her forty-two. His words were sweet but few. "Miss you so, much babe! Things are crazy here, but I'll call soon." That's the most she ever got.

When she could stand it no more, she started doing things she swore she never would, things she had seen her friends do, things she had seen on reality television. She sent angry texts. She called several times in a row. When he still didn't pick up, she started leaving voicemails.

The first voicemails sounded like this: "Honey, I know you're busy, but I really miss you and you're kind of freaking me out. I haven't talked to you in over two weeks, and it's making me sad. I don't want to bother you or anything, but I'm just so used to talking to you, and going this long without hearing from you is a really difficult change. I'm not trying to pressure you, sweetie, but if you could make some time to call me I would really appreciate it."

After three weeks without hearing from Justin, the voicemails started sounding like this: "So you just fuck me and leave me, is that it? Was that the whole point of our relationship? Did you find some slut to bang up there, so you don't need me anymore? You are a coward. You are a little bitch who can't handle a serious relationship."

Mia had never used words like that before, and the ease at which they flew from her mouth frightened her. She would always call back right away and apologize, though sometimes the apologies went on and on until she became angry and started swearing again. Mia was ashamed of herself, but she couldn't stop.

In psychological terms, Mia was starting to fragment. Parts of her identity were flying off in different directions. She loved Justin, but she also hated him for neglecting her. She hated herself for hating him, and she hated herself for loving him. Most people think they are above such behavior, but it's both typical and understandable in situations like this.

Mia's reality rested on the idea that Justin loved her. He had to love her, just like gravity had to keep her feet on the ground. A critical part of her self-worth depended on Justin's love. She also believed she had lost part of herself to him when they had sex. That only made sense in a world where Justin was crazy in love with her, and he had given her every reason to believe that. When Justin began ignoring her, the foundation of Mia's reality disappeared. Gravity stopped working. The world no longer made sense. In response to such insanity, her behavior followed suit.

Mia started missing school. She stopped taking care of herself. Her parents tried to ask her what was wrong, but she hid from them in her room. Finally, Justin called her almost two months after he had left for college.

The conversation was short but horrible. Justin said he couldn't be in a committed relationship while he was trying to "find himself."

Though he insisted that he had not been with anyone else, he said that he was going through a "seeking" phase. Then he chastised Mia for her vitriolic voicemails, as if he had done nothing to provoke them. In other words, Justin said all the self-absolving crap a college guy says after having a summer fling with a high school girl that's only about sex. When Justin told Mia that he still wanted to be friends, she hung up on him.

Depression flooded in. Mia told her mother that she had the flu. After a week in bed watching bad television and listening to the most melancholy indie folk she could find, she downed an energy drink and dragged herself back to school.

Word spread fast among the male populace that Mia no longer had a boyfriend. Boys started asking her out again. Unless the boy was repulsive, she said yes. If the boy could keep her interest long enough to make it to the third date, she had sex with him. Well, oral sex. She wouldn't have sexual intercourse unless they had been dating for at least a couple of months.

She enjoyed it sometimes. She became better at sex even if most of the boys didn't. She learned what she liked and told them how to do it. She always practiced safe sex. She focused on the physical pleasure. She didn't get any emotional satisfaction, but it made her feel wanted.

"I was not a stupid girl," Mia told me during one of our sessions. "I did well in school. I got accepted to USC with a partial academic scholarship. I was smart, so I don't know why it made sense to me at the time. I just figured I was damaged goods. I had already lost my virginity, so what was the point in not having sex? If you can't get the gift back, you might as well have sex, right? It sounds so ridiculous when I say it now. I wasn't trying to rationalize my behavior; it's what I really thought. I don't know how I could have believed something so ridiculous."

*****

I know how.

You can lose your integrity and get it back.

You can lose your courage and get it back.

You can lose compassion and get it back.

You can lose [fill in the blank] and get it back.

We don't think of most virtues as something we can lose. The last time you told a lie, you probably didn't think, "Oh no! I just lost my integrity!" The last time you failed to give to the needy, you probably didn't think, "My compassion is gone!" Instead, you saw it as a mistake. You committed a sin. You repented and *returned* to being honest or compassionate or whatever.

We don't treat sexual purity that way. Some attempts, like the "soul virgin" movement, promote the idea of recovering spiritual virginity, but even that is different from how we think of most virtues. We tend to see our virtues as part of our identity. We lapse from them but don't lose them. I've never heard of someone becoming "soul compassionate."

Let's do a little test. Do you think people should save sex for marriage? I do. If you're an Evangelical Christian, you probably do, too. Now, tell me where it says that in the Bible. It's a signature Christian belief, so book, chapter, and verse should leap from your brain, just like John 3:16.

I'm waiting . . .

(By the way, most New Testament scholars agree that "fornication" and "sexual immorality" mean adultery or sex with a prostitute) (Fiorenza, 1993).

Still waiting . . .

If you remembered something, I'm guessing it was something about general sexual purity. That's good stuff, but I'm interested in an explicit verse that says people should not have sex before marriage. Try again. This time, you have permission to use any resource at your disposal. Go Google your head off.

Finished? Great. Now find one that doesn't apply only to women.

I probably should have told you that there isn't one, but I didn't want you to take my word for it. I wanted you to see for yourself that not a single verse in the Bible prohibits premarital sex for everyone.

I'm not playing dialectical games with Scripture. For a long time, I sought such a verse in earnest. I spent over twenty years reading commentaries, exegeting passages, and translating the original languages trying to find a Biblical passage that forbids premarital sex. I wanted to find one but couldn't. But I'm not being legalistic either. The prohibition probably didn't need to be written down because it was common knowledge in both Old and New Testament Hebrew culture. It's also hard to walk away from passages like 1 Corinthians Chapters 6 and 7 believing that sex outside of marriage is okay. Like I said, I believe sex should be saved for marriage. I did this little exercise to point out that our preoccupation with virginity isn't rooted in a Biblical emphasis on abstinence. The emphasis comes from the secular world, not the Bible.

Until about the eighteenth century in Western culture, marriage was more about money and maintaining bloodlines than love (Bailey, 2004). In exchange for a fair dowry, a groom took a bride from a family of similar social standing. He provided for her financially and, in return, she managed his household and bore his children. The last thing the groom wanted was to raise another man's child, so it was essential for him to marry a virgin. Even if she lost her virginity long before marriage, she was "damaged goods" and unfit for any respectable man.

Though marriage is no longer an explicit financial arrangement in Western culture, we emphasize virginity more for girls than we do for boys. The archetypal virgin is feminine. In 2008 alone, there were over 1,400 "Purity Balls" at which girls made a vow to their father to remain chaste until he gave her away in marriage (Bersamin, et al., 2005). No such event exists for boys, at least not on the same scale. Even the dictionary on my Mac defines a virgin as "typically female." This why Christian men usually feel a little guilt for losing their virginity, while an avalanche of shame buries Christian women. Virginity becomes a dividing line in their identity. On one side, they are good girls. On the other, they are whores. This black-and-white approach to virginity makes women prizes to be "given away" in marriage rather than whole children of God.

Mia's beliefs about sexual purity grew out of a lie. They weren't based on Biblical wisdom. The Old Testament contains some of the oldest texts, by thousands of years, that extol the virtues of marriage and sex for love alone. The Song of Songs celebrates sexuality and love in their own right. Proverbs gives advice about pleasure and restraint in sex and marriage. In Corinthians, Paul tells us that sexuality is like eating, an important part of our being that needs love and care. Nowhere does the Bible say we can lose sexual purity forever. It definitely does not say that a woman's virginity is a commodity that can be damaged and devalued.

Yes, Mia should have waited until marriage to have sex. But identifying that as *the* problem with her sexuality would be like yelling at someone for eating ice cream after silently watching them devour two plates of chicken wings, a bucket of cheese fries, two pitchers of beer, and three cheeseburgers. Mia's sexuality was broken and bleeding long before she had sex.

First, Mia regarded her sexuality as something outside herself. It never felt like part of her. Second, it couldn't be good without being bad at the same time. If it brought her attention, her parents shamed her for it. If the boys liked it, they too often tried to take advantage of her. If it brought her pleasure, she felt ashamed. She had no sense of a sexuality that was hers, created by God. It should have been a stable part of her identity as a woman and a child of God. She should have had a sense of beauty that didn't depend on compliments or advances from males. If she felt that her sexuality was good and foundational, she would have recognized the dangers in her relationship with Justin long before his hands began to wander. In fact, she probably never would have dated him in the first place.

But the loss of virginity was all that mattered to Mia, her family, and her church. That made healing the rest of her sexuality far more difficult.

*****

By the time Mia was a high school senior, the guilt over losing her virginity subsided. As long as she was careful and didn't get emotionally involved, occasional sex was fun. She was smart about it and never had a pregnancy scare or caught a STD. She broke hearts more often than hers was broken. Sex didn't scare her anymore.

That changed when she went to college. Mia thought she was accustomed to attention from men. Her first month as a college freshman obliterated that notion. College boys flocked around her. When upperclassmen displaced the sweet freshmen boys she met at orientation, she found herself face to face with men in their mid-twenties offering her alcohol and inviting her back to their apartments off campus. It scared her at first, and she stuck with the girls in her dorm whenever she went to parties.

She relaxed once she started experimenting with alcohol. She'd had a beer now and then in high school, but she'd never been drunk. Fraternity parties featured sweet, colorful concoctions that went down faster and easier. Soon, she found herself laughing and flirting with the men lined up to meet her. She kissed strangers in dark hallways. When her roommate worried, Mia told her it was "all just good college fun."

On a Sunday morning in November, a buzzing vibration on Mia's thigh stirred her from sleep. When she opened her eyes, bright light shot through her retinas and burned her brain. She pressed a hand to her forehead, as if she could push away the hammers pounding her skull. The taste of bile filled her parched mouth. She forced her eyes open as they adjusted to the light. The room was too large. The walls were white and bare instead of the gentle green she and her roommate had chosen.

Where am I? As she pushed herself up, she touched flesh that wasn't hers and screamed. Next to her, a man with sandy blonde hair groaned and rolled away from her. He was naked.

She had no idea who he was. Then memories started to emerge through the fog of her hangover. His name was Rick. He was a graduate student or a law student, she couldn't remember which. The last thing she recalled was laughing with him outside of a fraternity party. She didn't remember coming to his apartment.

Mia reached down between her legs and knew right away what had happened. She shook Rick until he opened his eyes and looked at her.

"Did you use a condom?" she asked, though she already knew the answer.

"What's going on? Is the building on fire?"

"Just answer the question! Did you use a condom?"

The man rubbed his eyes. "I don't think so. Probably not. You mean you're not on the pill or anything?"

Her body sounded alarms that she was about to vomit, but she held it back. "Why would you do that to me?" Mia shouted.

"It's not a big deal. Just get a morning-after pill or something," said Rick. Then he rolled over like he was going back to sleep.

Mia dashed to the bathroom and threw up. Rick managed to get out of bed and offer her some water. She pushed past him and gathered her scattered things. She got dressed as fast as she could and fled the apartment.

When she got outside, she saw a tree-lined street of apartment buildings that she didn't recognize. She checked her location using her phone: Pasadena, twenty minutes from campus. Her roommate could pick her up. If not, she'd eat the thirty-dollar cab ride.

She started to call her roommate. That's when she noticed the missed calls: seven of them, all from her mother. She checked the time: 2:17 p.m. When her parents complained about not seeing her enough, she had agreed to meet them for lunch today. They set it up two weeks ago.

Mia dropped her phone, and it bounced off the sidewalk. She collapsed on the curb, buried her head in her arms, and began to cry. She began praying, really praying, for the first time in years. Most of what she said was, "Help." She felt the answer like a whisper from within, "Ask for help and it will come."

Who do I ask? Not her parents. They would just freak out. Not anyone from her old church. They would freak out, too. She picked up her phone and did a search on the first three words that came to mind:

God, sex, counseling. My name, next to a picture of my gigantic noggin, was on the first page of results.

I guess he'll do, thought Mia. *Better act before I lose my nerve.* She called and left a voicemail at my office.

We had our first appointment the following week. She would be my client for the next five years.

*****

As a psychotherapist, the people you enjoy working with the most can also frustrate you the most. I liked working with Mia. She was bright, pleasant, and funny. She always showed up for her appointments on time. I looked forward to seeing her every week, but she also gave me reasons to worry about her every week.

Mia made a few positive changes at first. Like too many college students, she had learned the hard way that binge drinking and sex mix about as well as fire and gasoline. She curtailed her alcohol consumption. She began examining her motivations for having sex, though she didn't stop all together. She wouldn't sleep with a man unless he was officially her boyfriend.

The fact that she was still having sex didn't bother me as much as her judgment when it came to bequeathing the title of "boyfriend." Though she talked about improving her self-esteem in our sessions, her judgment reflected little change. The men she chose would ply her with shallow romantic overtures until she agreed to date them. Then they would have a lot of sex. Next, the guy would break up with her after no more than a few months, if not weeks. We spent the majority of our time in therapy patching the emotional holes left by these relationships. Her boyfriends in college were all bad sequels to Justin.

So when she got engaged to the actual Justin, it was all I could do not to shout, "Are you out of your mind?"

After Justin graduated from college in Seattle, he returned to LA and got a job as a production assistant ("PA") for a Hollywood movie studio. A PA is a glorified internship. If you land one, you're supposed to feel lucky for getting an entry-level job in "the industry." You sacrifice a living wage and a humane schedule for the opportunity to fetch coffee and run errands for someone with keys to the cinematic kingdom.

Justin went from being a campus big shot to a Hollywood peon. He spent long days with people being rude to him and lonely nights living at home with his parents. It didn't take long for him to seek out Mia.

She didn't make it easy for him. His penance included a "friendship" period during which he had to regain Mia's trust. Mia said they weren't dating, but, to me, it sounded just like dating with a kissing ban, the opposite of friends with benefits.

"Justin has really changed," Mia told me.

"It sounds like you're starting to trust him a lot more," I said.

"He's worked hard for it," she said.

I just nodded.

You might be wondering why I didn't cut the therapist crap and tell Mia to kick Justin to the curb (or kick him somewhere else). That doesn't always work, and it definitely wouldn't have worked with Mia. Romantic attention from men provided Mia with what some psychologists call a "sense of self." During the brief periods when she didn't have a man in her life, she would sink into a depression peppered with spikes of anxiety. She lost herself. It went deeper than simple cognitive exercises such as, "What do you like about yourself?" Mia could tell me what she liked about herself. She could identify strengths that had nothing to do with being attractive to men. But without a man's attention, she could not *feel* good, no matter what she thought. A man's affection anchored her to herself. When she had a boyfriend, she got good grades, exercised, spent time with her friends, and even went to church. Without a man, life overwhelmed and terrified her.

Once I lost patience and let it slip that I thought she was making a mistake by reconnecting with Justin. She just agreed with me and changed the subject, as if I'd told her that I liked Disneyland. Had I pressed Mia to leave Justin, she never would have done it. If I pressed too hard, she would have stopped coming to therapy. Until her sense of identity and value rested on something other than romance, my job was to walk beside her on this path. When she fell, I helped her stand up again. Telling Mia she was on the wrong path was pointless. She was going to have to discover that on her own. I just wish it hadn't taken so long and hurt so much.

*****

Justin and Mia got engaged less than three months after he reentered her life. They got married almost six years to the day after they met. As the wedding drew near, even I started coming around to the idea that Justin had changed. Maybe a fairy tale ending wasn't out of the question.

Mia had insisted that they refrain from sex until their wedding night. It was Justin's final step in rebuilding trust. She and Justin became active in a small but vibrant faith community in Hollywood, filled with mostly "industry" types seeking shelter among other Christians. They attended a small group every week. Their pastor gave them premarital counseling. Every week, Mia showed up at my office eager to share the latest touching story. It was a time of hope and excitement.

Mia had only two concerns as the big day approached: her weight and the wedding night. Over the last two years, Mia had gained a few pounds. I thought she needed the extra weight. Had she been any thinner, I would have raised concerns about an eating disorder. Justin teased her about gaining weight once but stopped after he saw the tears. Her mother, however, did a lot more than tease.

The more I learned about Mia's family, the more I understood why her sense of value was tied to being attractive. Her parents had raised her to believe that securing a good husband was the path to happiness and stability. For her father, this was about picking a solvent man with good business sense. For her mother, it meant being pretty enough to snag such a man. But her mother's advice always had a narcissistic edge.

"I don't remember my skin having so many blemishes at your age," Mia's mother said when Mia was thirteen. "You should wear more make up or the boys will think you have a disease."

When Mia was in high school her mother told her, "You get a lot of attention from boys, but that's just because you're such a flirt. I was pretty enough that I could be a good girl and still get the boys."

Whenever I thought Mia's mother could no longer surprise me, Mia would come to therapy with reports of a nasty new one-liner that made my jaw drop.

After Mia finished the final fitting for her wedding dress, she texted her mother, excited to share the news. Seconds later, her phone lit up with her mother's reply.

"I'm just glad they could make it fit you after all the weight you've gained. I think you have your proof that Justin doesn't just love you for your body anymore!" Smiley face. Wink.

Though Justin assured her that she was more beautiful than ever, Mia cried herself to sleep that night. It was all I could do to keep her from going on a crazy fast diet before the wedding. Frustrated, I sidelined empathy in favor of confrontation and presented Mia with a choice: "You can look healthy and happy on your wedding day or shed a few pounds that no one but your mom will notice and faint during your vows," I said. "It's up to you."

Mia decided against the fainting.

Mia's other worry concerned the wedding night. When she dated Justin as a teenager, Mia had fantasized about their wedding night. Now she approached it with dread, obsessing over a single fear: that she could not have sex with Justin without having "flashbacks" of all the other men she had slept with.

When she told me that, it pissed me off almost as much as her mom's comments about her weight, but I kept my cool. "What gave you that idea?" I asked, though I could guess.

"It's just what I've always heard," said Mia.

"Where?"

"I don't know," she said. "In church growing up, I guess."

Yeah, I thought, *that's where I heard it, too.*

*****

The story goes like this: You become emotionally and spiritually tied to someone when you have sex with that person. As a result, whenever you sleep with someone new, all your previous partners end up in bed with you. It's like a paranormal orgy. Newlyweds who don't save sex for marriage risk having "flashbacks" about previous partners on their wedding night, making the magical night potentially traumatic.

Ladies and gentlemen, this is bullshit at its purest. Nothing, not one word of Scripture and not one shred of scientific evidence validates this folklore. People don't think about other people during sex on their wedding night. If they do, they have much deeper problems than the fact that they had premarital sex. Something about intimacy frightens them, or they have some kind of psychological disorder.

Or maybe they couldn't get the idea out of their head because someone told them it would happen.

The message that you will mentally revisit past lovers on your wedding night is not just untrue. It's worse than a lie It's a trap. By telling young people that this kind of thing happens, it plants a suggestion in their minds. It could actually make something happen that *would not happen otherwise.* In other words, if you had sex before marriage and couldn't keep visions of past sexual partners out of your head, it probably happened because someone told you that it would.

Yes, I'm saying that it's not your fault.

*****

Mia didn't think about anyone but Justin on her wedding night or any other night of the honeymoon. Her only regret was using credit cards to pay for a trip to Maui, because they hardly left the hotel room. She said they could have gone to a Motel Six in Fresno and had almost the identical honeymoon.

The first month of their marriage was more of the same: lots of sex and lots of fun. When Justin got hired to work on a movie, they saw less of each other, but it wasn't a problem. Mia had a new job at an advertising agency, so she was busy, too. They spent time together at night and on the weekends. When Justin spent more and more time on his computer, Mia assumed he was working on one of his screenplays. His dream was to write and direct films, and she wasn't about to stand in his way.

She tried not to complain when he stayed up late in front of his laptop. Sex dropped from every night to once or twice a week, but it only bothered her a little. When it fell to less than once a week, she told herself that a steep drop in sex was normal during the first year of marriage. When Justin stopped touching her altogether, she had to say something. "I want us to be intimate more often," she said to Justin one night as he sat in his usual trance in front of his laptop.

"I would like to be more intimate, too," he said without looking up. "Maybe you could start going to the gym or something. It would be easier to get turned on if you lost a little chunk."

Mia felt dizzy and her hands started to shake. He had never said anything so cruel. Unable to speak, she dashed into the bedroom and shut the door. Justin didn't follow her. He didn't come to bed until long after she'd fallen into a morose, fitful sleep. When she got home from work the next day, Justin was in the shower. His computer sat open on the kitchen table.

Don't do it, she thought. *You are not that woman.*

The impulse was too strong. She sat down and opened his web browser. Her job was in online advertising, and she was far more adept at peeking into someone's online activity than Justin knew. She was expecting porn. What she found was worse.

Justin had been chatting with a girl he knew in college. No, not chatting, commiserating. Complaining about his marriage. He expressed regret, but not just about getting married. He regretted that this skinny blonde vixen had a boyfriend in college so he never had the chance to date her. He and this woman, who looked like a Midwestern crystal meth addict, were fantasizing about what it would be like to be *married to each other.*

Mia picked up the computer and went into the bathroom. Justin was still in the shower. She threw it as hard as she could at the wall just above his head. It shattered, ricocheting all over the shower, and all over Justin. He was still cursing and screaming as she walked out of the apartment, slamming the door behind her.

*****

Mia and Justin had been married less than a year when they got divorced. That's better than being married for years and having kids, but I didn't tell her that. It wouldn't have helped.

Mia's depression and anxiety took control. I consulted with a medical colleague, who prescribed antidepressants to stabilize her mood. The medication helped her function and go to work, but she was still miserable. The pinnacle of fulfillment and happiness in her life had been marriage. Marrying the man who had once rejected her was the ultimate victory. When he again rejected her for someone else, making a crack about her weight in the process, it was a defeat worse than death. I mean that literally: Mia often talked about suicide, though she promised never to do it. Only increasing our sessions to three times a week and adding new medications kept her out of the hospital. I seldom take my work home with me, but I lost several nights of sleep worrying that Mia would break her promise and take her own life.

Working with her in therapy during that time was like sitting in a tomb. When she wasn't crying, she didn't know what to say. Nothing in life stimulated her, nothing gave her joy. Though she was still attractive, she was no longer a vortex for male attention. She felt like she no longer existed. In therapy, it felt like trying to call Lazarus back from the dead.

Raising someone from the dead is way above my pay grade, not to mention my skill set. That's Someone else's job.

*****

Mia lay on the floor staring at the ceiling. She cradled the bottle of vodka in her arms like a baby. The bottle of pills was on the kitchen counter. She wasn't sure about the pills yet, but she was sure about the vodka. She would puke if she drank the whole bottle, but half of it would make her pass out. She would regret it when she woke up tomorrow, unless she took the pills. Then she wouldn't wake up at all.

If nothing else, she needed some ice and a glass, maybe a lime. No reason self-destruction should taste like rubbing alcohol. She bumped into a bookcase as she stood up. A book fell out and landed at her feet. She picked it up to put it back in place and read the cover: *The Return of the Prodigal Son: A Story of Homecoming* by Henri J.M. Nouwen. I had loaned it to her over a year ago, saying she could keep it as long as she wanted. She had forgotten about the book and felt guilty for keeping it for so long. Her chagrin at still having the book was the only thing that made her open it. She only meant to read a few pages. She sat on the floor and crossed her legs, the bottle vodka resting unopened in her lap.

Many of Nouwen's words brought tears to her eyes, but this is the passage made her collapse to the floor, weeping.

> *Now I wonder whether I have sufficiently realized that during all this time God has been trying to find me, to know me, and to love me. The question is not "How am I to find God?" but "How am I to let myself be found by him?" The question is not "How am I to know God?" but "How am I to let myself be known by God?" And, finally, the question is not "How am I to love God?" but "How am I to let myself be loved by God?" God is looking into the distance for me, trying to find me, and longing to bring me home* (Nouwen, 2016, p. 54.

Mia had known that God loved her for as long as she could remember, but this was the first time she ever *felt* loved by God. God had always loved her, but she had been unable to feel any love that wasn't wrapped up in shame and conditions. Mia did not understand it, but she felt it.

Mia kept reading until she finished the book at 5 a.m. She was still in pain. She still didn't know who she was. But she felt loved, and it had nothing to do with pleasing a man or her mother. It had nothing to do with being a virgin or not. She was God's beloved. That was all that mattered. That was enough. She put the vodka away, made coffee, and got ready for work.

*****

When Mia started an online publishing company, I didn't tell her about the people I knew who had done the same thing and failed. I want to support my clients when they're excited about something. But that wasn't my only reason for not telling Mia. I didn't tell her any cautionary tales because I knew she could make it work. Mia had always been bright and industrious. Her professors raved about her writing skills.

When she got a job in advertising out of college, she discovered a natural talent for web design. Her abilities — not her looks — got her noticed by important people. Her genial personality and quick wit made networking fun instead of a chore.

For most of her life, Mia's gifts never mattered to her. She only cared about what mattered to others, whether it was sex, chastity, or avoiding her mother's scorn. Validation based on the standards of others was her emotional oxygen, so she didn't care about her own talents and what she wanted to do with them. When God showed her that she was beloved by His standards and nothing could change that, everything changed.

Mia started an online magazine for women while she was still working full time in advertising. She quit her job after two other magazines took off, and she had a steady stream of income. She handled almost everything herself for the first year, but now she has a staff of eight. She makes big decisions and leaves most of the details to others, but she still writes a weekly column. Her favorite topics are body image, faith, and self-esteem for women.

Mia is still my client, though she goes months without an appointment. When she hits a rough patch, she'll come back for a month or two. For some people, therapy is a one-time effort that ends with a final farewell. But a lot of my clients, like Mia, never really say goodbye. We do tough work for a while and then they come back to therapy when they need it. It's having a dentist, with less pain and more talking.

When Mia returns to therapy, she seldom talks about men. She talks about work. She talks about the future and what she wants to give to the world. For about a year after her night in God's embrace via Henri Nouwen, Mia was intent on rebuilding her life without romance. She learned how to love life and herself. When the subject of men comes up, it's because a guy asked her out and she has to suppress a knee-jerk reaction that he's a lecherous Lothario that she should kick in the groin.

Mia has old wounds that will take time to heal. Her sexuality is battered and bruised but no longer broken. It now resides in her sense of womanhood, a fundamental part of her female humanity. She might share that with a man again someday. He'll have to work for it, but so will she. She will have to find a way for sexuality and romantic love to intertwine without shame.

As for sexual purity and her long-lost virginity, Mia thinks in different terms now. "I don't see myself having sex again before marriage," she told me during one session. "I don't see the point. I can imagine sex being fun again, but I want a lot more than that. I used to think sex was such a big deal, but it's just the tip of the iceberg. I'm going to be worried about a lot more than sex the next time I fall in love."

She grew quiet and looked down. "I suffered a lot for a long time because I thought sex was so important. Because I thought giving or getting sex was important. Because I thought being a virgin or not was so important. I don't want to think like that anymore. I like to think I was never a virgin or not a virgin; I was just a person that God loved. I made a lot of mistakes because I didn't feel that love, but I feel it now. As long as I hold on to that love, I'm not so worried about making mistakes."

Tears rose to my eyes. Mia noticed and smiled. This smile hid nothing, radiating warmth and beauty from inside and out.

Chapter Four:
Becky & Patrick

Becky and Patrick came to see me after being married for just over a year. They wanted therapy for the same reason that many Christian newlyweds do: They had both remained virgins until their wedding night, but sex hadn't been working out the way they had hoped.

Couples come to me for sexual problems all the time. But a distinct despair hangs over Christian newlyweds that save sex for marriage, only to discover something other than marathon love-making and orgasmic bliss on the other side of their wedding vows. Before marriage, they white-knuckle their way past desire to touch each other in intimate ways because they believe that the most powerful physical bond should be preserved for the most holy commitment. I think it's right, noble, and admirable.

What is neither noble nor admirable, however, is the reward some married Christians promise unmarried Christians in return for chastity. Singles hear tales of unbridled sexual ecstasy awaiting those that survive the trials of abstinence. Married Christians dangle the wedding night like a carrot in front of a tired, sweaty, sexually pure stallion. Such a message is not Biblical, scientific, or wise. Christian culture sets the bar so high for newly married sex that disappointment is all but inevitable.

The good news is that the damage is usually easy to repair. When I meet a couple that's disappointed with their first sexual encounters, a little education gets them back on track. Five lessons surprise and relieve most couples:

1) Though sex can be emotionally powerful the first time, it's not always filled with physical funzies, especially for the ladies. There's a good chance it will hurt.

2) Symbolically, the wedding night is the perfect time to have sex for the first time. Practically, it's one of the worst occasions imaginable to have sex for the first time. A wedding is one of the biggest events of your life. It's emotionally and physically exhausting, but you won't

know it until you arrive at the honeymoon suite and your adrenaline takes a nosedive. You will suddenly notice how dehydrated you are. The bride will have had the longer day and be far more tired than the groom. That big, beautiful bed might arouse nothing more than lust for sleep. Despite all this, the couple feels pressured to do something for the first time that is both emotionally intense and physically delicate. And they expect it to be spectacular.

3) Good sex requires practice and patience. Sex gets better the more you do it, but it's usually not very good at first. Sex is like every other aspect of a long-term relationship: It requires a willingness to learn about yourself and your partner.

4) About fifty percent (50%) of all women cannot orgasm through sexual intercourse. If couples are not aware of this, it sets them up for two major pitfalls. First, the woman will be disappointed with sex and might even feel like something is wrong with her. Second, the husband will feel pressured to maintain an erection without ejaculating for as long as possible as he tries to go longer and longer in the hope of finally providing his wife with an orgasm. If a couple doesn't understand that they might need to explore other ways for the woman to reach orgasm, sex can start to feel laborious. They might even start to avoid it.

5) Success in sex cannot be defined by orgasm. This is the most important point and the most difficult one to drive home. Our culture, including Christian culture, over-simplifies physical intimacy and sexual pleasure. If couples can learn how to enjoy physical intimacy without making it all about orgasm, it lowers everyone's anxiety. Problems such as performance anxiety, difficulty reaching orgasm, premature ejaculation, and other common complications become less worrisome if earth-shattering climax isn't a requirement for every intimate moment.

As I explain these things to newlyweds, the tension begins to leak out of the room. Once they learn that their problems are normal, everyone relaxes. After a few weeks of massaging wounds and trying new things, our work is done.

But that wasn't enough for Becky and Patrick. The wounds were too old and too deep.

*****

Becky and Patrick broke a rule the first time they held hands. Brother Wayne, their youth pastor, always told them, only "brief, appropriate side-hugs" were allowed between boys and girls at Helena Baptist Church.

Still, Becky couldn't help herself. She had dated Patrick for three months and hardly touched him, even though she had never felt so attracted to someone. She hadn't always felt that way, not really. No one would argue that Patrick was good-looking, with his broad shoulders, sandy hair, and rugged but smart features. She just had always assumed that he was dumb, like every other guy who played two sports, especially if one of them was football. It only took two conversations for her to find out that Patrick was far from stupid, but that didn't happen until they had been alone. She'd started dropping references to Shakespeare and Robert Frost to see if he could keep up. Patrick saw her Frost and Shakespeare, then raised with T.S. Eliot and Walt Whitman. Becky was hooked.

She hadn't planned on holding Patrick's hand that night, three months later. They were sitting in the balcony during the Sunday evening service. His hand had been close to hers. The urge she had to touch him was strong. She slid her hand under his, and he instantly wrapped his fingers around it. *For the football win!* she thought. She didn't smile because she didn't want to draw attention. That didn't stop Patrick from smiling. Becky felt a tingle in her abdomen. She liked it but willed it away. She didn't want to get in trouble. Holding hands was already a big risk.

At a church lock-in three years previously, about a dozen youth group members snuck off to the basement to play "spin the bottle." Someone found out about it and snitched. Brother Wayne responded with a new set of rules that banned any form of physical contact with romantic intent. The list of forbidden behaviors was long: It included kissing, cuddling, hand-holding, full-frontal hugging, back rubs, foot rubs, slow dancing, fast dancing, and the deadly "other inappropriate behaviors." The last item meant that Wayne could decide that anything was off limits if he deemed it "inappropriate."

For a blessed fifteen minutes, Patrick and Becky forgot about Brother Wayne's list and enjoyed holding hands. When the service ended, they withdrew their hands and stuffed them in their pockets. They trotted down the stairs of the balcony and toward the exit, as if fleeing the scene of a crime.

In the vestibule, Patrick gave Becky an "appropriate" side hug. He wanted to kiss her, but he knew better. It wasn't just Brother Wayne's rules. Like Becky, he was trying to behave himself. They were trying to focus on the friendship, the emotional and spiritual side of the relationship. Though they were virgins, they had both done a lot of kissing in past relationships, and they were trying to remain pure and keep the focus on Christ. It had been a little easier for Patrick than Becky. Patrick said it was because Becky didn't have three hours of basketball practice to burn off the extra sexual energy. Becky didn't think that was true, but she thought Patrick was a sweetie for saying so.

Patrick headed for the parking lot to drive home. Becky had to wait for her mother, who was helping out in the nursery. They said a restrained goodbye, and Becky began to walk back through the sanctuary toward the nursery.

"Rebecca," said a voice from behind. Her stomach did a flip.

"Hi, Brother Wayne," she said, turning around.

"Hey, there. Got a minute?"

"Well, I need to meet my mom."

"She'll be busy in the nursery for at least another 20 minutes. We need to talk."

Crap.

"Okay, sure," said Becky, trying to sound cheerful.

They went into Wayne's office, and he shut the door. Wayne didn't waste any time.

"I see you and Patrick are getting pretty close," he said.

"I reckon so," said Becky.

"You guys seemed to take things to the next level tonight."

How could he have seen us holding hands? Does he have cameras in the balcony? I wouldn't put it past him.

Becky knew better than to deny anything, but she wasn't going to outright confess, either.

"I just really like him," she said.

"I can see that," said Wayne. "But a pretty girl like you has to be careful. Patrick is good guy, but he's still a *guy*. A guy's hormones can get out of control, and that can mean trouble for a pretty girl like you."

Becky was pretty sure that she could be just as much trouble for Patrick as the other way around, but she wasn't about to tell Wayne that.

"I appreciate you holding us accountable" said Becky, and she meant it—at least a little. "But we've been doing a really good job. We both want things to be different than in our past relationships. We've been keeping the focus on friendship and on God."

Wayne said nothing for a moment and then smiled.

"I am so glad to hear that," he said. "Have you read Elisabeth Elliot's book?"

"I've heard of it," said Becky.

Wayne got up and went to his bookshelf. He slid out a thin paperback book and tossed it on the table in front of Becky. The title was *Passion and Purity*. On the cover was a guy hiding flowers behind his back. Becky wondered what that had to do with passion or purity. Were the flowers dangerous or something?

"You can have that copy if you promise me that you'll read it," said Wayne.

"I'll try. School keeps me pretty busy, so it might be a while."

"You're such a great student, I don't see how you do it," said Wayne. "I could barely keep a 3.0. But this is important."

"Patrick reads a lot," said Becky. "Maybe I'll let him take a crack at it first."

"No," said Wayne. "I want you to read it, not Patrick. Just trust me on this."

"Okay," she said. It was an odd request, but she'd been taught long ago to respect her elders, especially church leadership.

"Thanks for your time," said Wayne. "I know that God has mighty things in store for you. You're going to make some man very happy someday, and I don't want to see you toss aside something precious before God's chosen time."

They stood up. Wayne spread his arms for a hug and Becky obliged. She let go before he did.

"I'll see you on Wednesday," he said.

"Thanks," said Becky. "See you later, Brother Wayne."

It wasn't until she was halfway home, listening to her mother tell nursery horror stories, that it hit her. Wayne never said a word about her holding hands with Patrick.

*****

"Where were you tonight in church?" Patrick's mother asked as soon as he walked through the door.

"I was sitting in the balcony," said Patrick, and kept moving toward his room. He knew where this was going, and he had homework to finish.

"You were with that girl, weren't you?" she said.

"She has a name, mom."

"Well, if you are going to sit with *Rebecca* instead of your parents, I would prefer that you sit downstairs where everyone can see you. You don't want to give people the wrong impression."

"By going to church on Sunday night with my girlfriend?"

"Don't talk back to your mother like that. You know what I mean. The two of you have been spending a lot of time together."

Patrick knew he was on thin ice, but he had grown weary of innuendos and veiled invectives.

"We are not having sex, mom. And we're not going to unless we get married."

His mother's head went back and her mouth opened. But she recovered quickly, her eyes growing cold. "Good," she said. "Because I'd rather you become a crackhead than give in to your carnal urges."

Someone else might have thought his mother was using hyperbole, but Patrick knew better. He had come home drunk from a party during his freshman year, and his mother had been waiting for him. She did no more than shake her head as he stumbled through the door and into the bathroom, where a river of Bud Light vacated his stomach by way of his mouth. But when she had caught him looking at Internet pornography for the first and last time in his life, she became hysterical. She declared him a "wicked person" and that the "devil had taken hold" of him. She took a hammer to his laptop and tossed it into the trash (though, unbeknownst to her, she had only shattered the monitor and he had been able to salvage the hard drive and hours of homework). Patrick had little doubt that his mother would prefer that he succumb to drug addiction rather than his sexual urges.

"Goodnight, mom," said Patrick. "I have a lot of homework." Arguing with her was a lost cause. He went into his room and closed the door, careful not to slam it so he wouldn't get another reprimand.

Patrick finished his homework a lot faster than anyone, except Becky, realized that he could. Then he picked up his phone and sent Becky a text: "I think I love you." He was surprised that he didn't feel more nervous typing those words.

The reply came seconds later: "I don't think. I know."

Patrick responded with a smiley face. Then he turned out the lights and fell into a deep, unbroken sleep.

*****

If you ask most Christian adults what they think about two teenagers professing love for each other, you'll get an interesting array of reactions. The majority will probably shrug it off as cute and call it something like "puppy love." Most of us had a crush in high school that looks a little melodramatic in retrospect. A very solid, vocal minority will cite a profession of love during adolescence as cause for concern, perhaps alarm. They'll say teenagers don't have the maturity for serious relationships. What they usually mean by this is at that teenage love leads to teenage sex. Bringing up the rear will be a remnant of past generations who simply remark, "People got married when they were teenagers in my day."

You will seldom hear the Biblical reality and psychological science about teenage love: It's good. In the Bible, most people who fall in love are teenagers. Well, the girls are, anyway.

"But, wait!" you say, "That's because most marriages were arranged, and an older man marrying a teenage girl was part of Biblical culture."

To which I respond, "You are correct, sir or madam. Except for the Song of Songs, one of the oldest books in the Bible."

Then you say, "Isn't that the naughty book that some people call the Song of Solomon?"

Then I say, "Oh, yeah."

The Song of Songs is a poem about mutual courtship (and then some) between two "young" people. The woman is described as a girl. Ancient Hebrew culture was unique in that it valued romantic love as part of marriage and sex (Nelson, 1978). Until about the seventeenth or eighteenth century AD, almost every culture in the world viewed marriage as a financial arrangement and sex as a means of procreation and maintaining bloodlines (Nelson, 1978). The Old Testament Hebrews bucked the trend, and they did it as adolescents.

The psychology supporting the benefits of young love is simple: It's an important developmental task. It shows that you have the capacity for intimacy and attachment. You can take someone else in and make them important. Loving someone else can actually help solidify your own identity. Now, that last sentence may not make sense based on the number of people who seem to lose their identity in relationships, especially as teenagers. Unfortunately, that's part of the process of establishing your own identity. Sometimes we have to lose ourself a little bit in a relationship in order to discover and clarify the outline of our identity. For example, only by briefly losing myself in a relationship with a woman who loved French films did I discover that I can't stomach French films.

But there's something else important about falling in love as a teenager: It means you're more likely to make better decisions about sex. Ever since the sexual revolution made the combination of sex and commitment obsolete, adolescents and young adults can choose to have their first experience with intimacy in one of two ways: physical or emotional. Research shows that if someone's first experience with intimacy is emotional, they will make better decisions as adults (Shaughnessy and Shakesby, 1992). They will be less promiscuous and are more likely to be positive, helpful, and friendly.

In other words, if two young people who aren't having sex say they love each other, it means they're good kids.

Becky and Patrick were good. I wish all the adults in their lives had been just as good.

*****

"I think I love you."

When those words flashed across her phone, Becky had squealed, and she was *not* a girl that squealed. She didn't even have to think about the reply: "I don't think. I know."

When Patrick responded with smiley face, she giggled. When nothing else followed, she was a little disappointed. Couldn't he follow up with anything better than that? And why couldn't he have told her in person? But she was too happy to be upset with him.

She tossed and turned for hours, trying to sleep, but all she could think about was Patrick. She prayed and praised God. She prayed and asked God to guide them. She asked for wisdom.

Dream images shifted in and out of consciousness as she drifted off to sleep. Then her eyes popped open as the last lucid thought of the day made its appearance. It was so potent and vivid that she said it aloud. "I am going to kiss that boy," she said, then fell asleep.

*****

As usual, the heater in Patrick's Honda Civic didn't start to deliver until he reached the school parking lot. Monday mornings in February were the abyss of the school year. Friday was a long way off. Spring break was light years away. Christmas break was a distant memory. And the only thing awaiting him at the end of the day was basketball practice where Coach would feel free to run them to death since the next game was five days away. He wouldn't even see Becky until lunch.

But there she was. As he pulled into the parking lot, he saw her standing on the curb, waving. "Hi," he said, getting out of the car.

"Come with me. Hurry," she said.

"What's going on?"

"First period starts in six minutes, just hush and follow me. Quick."

"Fine," he said, rolling his eyes.

He took off after Becky, who was moving too fast for 6:54 am on a Monday morning. She led him around the left side of the school, toward the football field. She rounded the corner and kept going.

"Becky, my class is the other way. Can we talk —"

"Shh!"

She grabbed his hand and pulled him underneath the bleachers at the edge of the football field. Then she whirled around, grabbed the front of his letterman jacket, pulled him into her, and kissed him hard on the mouth.

Patrick overcame his astonishment in seconds. He dropped his book bag and put his arms around her. Her hand slid behind his head. Their lips moved soft and swift over each other. Patrick smelled soap and tasted Aquafresh. Their breath quickened. When Becky finally pulled away, a puff of steam went up between them in the chilly morning air. Patrick pulled her back and kissed her again. Then he stopped and hugged her close.

"That. Was. Awesome," he said.

Becky sighed. "Yeah."

Holding hands, they scurried back toward school. They were both tardy for class, but it was their first tardy of the year, so their teachers let it slide.

In the week after that first kiss, Becky and Patrick made out every time they were alone. Determined not to let "the flesh" dominate the relationship, Patrick established what he called the "The Three Laws" (Patrick was a big Isaac Asimov fan, but Becky didn't get it):

1) "We will make out only three times a week."
2) "We will make out for only thirty minutes at a time."
3) "Making out means kissing, cuddling, and clothing."

Patrick and Becky did an excellent job abiding by The Three Laws. Only twice did confusion arise.

The first time occurred during an all-night church ski trip. The youth group was night-skiing on lighted slopes when Becky suggested that she and Patrick sneak off to an isolated spot. She said that they should meet at 11:30 p.m. She kept reminding Patrick, saying, "Remember, we have to be there at exactly 11:30." When they met, they proceeded to cuddle and kiss for their usual thirty minutes.

When thirty minutes were up, Patrick said, "I guess we have to stop now."

"No, we don't," said Becky.

"Hun, I would love to do this all night, but we made a promise to each other."

"And I have every intention of keeping that promise. We began making out at 11:30 p.m. on Saturday night. It is now 12:00 a.m. on Sunday. It is a brand new day and a brand new week, so we can just start over again."

Patrick paused, shrugged, and said, "Okay."

The next week, they decided to add an amendment prohibiting the use of loopholes that allowed back-to-back make out sessions.

The second event was more complicated, and far more confusing. When they had been dating almost a year, Patrick and Becky were watching a movie at Becky's house while her parents were out to dinner. Becky's parents trusted her and didn't mind letting them have the house. Her father even teased her about having a free night to "smooch her boyfriend," which always made Becky go red and say, "Stop it, daddy!"

The movie was *Catwoman,* starring Halle Barry, and it was awful. They stopped paying attention after thirty minutes.

"Do you want to do something else?" asked Becky.

"I think we can figure out something for the next, oh, I don't know, half an hour."

"Excellent, idea, sir."

They started kissing, but something was different this time. The kissing was more intense, more passionate. Their hands did not wander, and they held each other tighter than usual. After about ten minutes, Becky started to feel warm. Her skin became sensitive, but in a way she liked. She went from feeling warm to feeling hot. Her breath quickened, and her body started to quiver. It scared her, but she didn't want it to stop. It was one of the best things she had ever felt in her life. The pleasure was intense, overwhelming. At last, it was too much, and she pulled away from Patrick.

"Stop, stop," she said, gasping. Patrick rolled away from her and faced the other direction. He buried his face in a pillow.

"What's wrong?" she asked.

"Nothing," said Patrick.

"Honey, are you okay? I didn't mean to hurt your feelings. I just–"

"It's fine. I just need to go home."

"Patrick! What is it?"

"Nothing. I just need to leave."

"Honey, turn around and look at me."

"No."

"What on earth is the matter with you?"

"It's . . . Can I just leave and tell you later?"

It hit her at once. "Oh my gosh," she said. "It happened to you too, didn't it?"

"Yes!" Patrick shouted. "That's why I need to go home right now!"

Becky slapped her hand over her mouth. She wasn't sure if she was horrified or about to burst out laughing. "Oh, baby," she said, "it's okay."

Patrick groaned, his face still stuffed into the pillow. "I know it's okay," he said, his voice muffled by the pillow. "But I have to change into the sweatpants in my gym bag before I go home, or my mom will kill me when she sees my pants. I also feel like a glazed donut right now, and it's kind of icky. So, for Pete's sake, can I please go deal with this situation?"

A laugh exploded from Becky.

"I am so going to kill you," said Patrick.

"I'm sorry honey, it's . . . it's not funny."

"Then stop laughing."

"I will, someday," she said and gave him a kiss on the cheek.

Patrick left to deal with his situation. Becky was still laughing when he drove away, but she stopped a moment later.

What was *that?*

Three hours later, she was pulling and kicking her sheets, as if they were the reason she couldn't sleep. She had tried praying, but she didn't know what to pray about. Had she done something wrong? She and Patrick didn't do anything other than kiss, and she had never felt conflicted about that. Regardless of what Brother Wayne said, nothing in the Bible convinced her that it was a sin to kiss your boyfriend. The thing that she felt tonight, however, felt so good and so bad at the same time. No, it was too complicated, too overwhelming for little words like "good" and "bad." She felt guilty about it, but she also really wanted it to happen again, and that made her feel even more guilty.

Another problem was that she wasn't exactly sure what *it* was. She assumed that she had an orgasm, but she thought that only happened during sex. That's what bothered her so much. If she and Patrick both had orgasms, then they must have crossed a line that displeased God.

Why did this happen, Lord? We weren't trying to make it happen. I don't understand this, and I need your help, because I hate feeling so bad and so good about something at the same time. It's driving me crazy.

Becky heard a clinking sound down the hallway, the unmistakable beacon of a midnight raid on the kitchen. She knew who it was. She tossed her feet over the side of the bed, stood up, and started down the hall toward the kitchen, fully aware that she might regret it for the rest of her life.

Her mom sat at the kitchen table, her back to Becky. She was eating fig newtons and reading something on her computer.

"Hi, mom," said Becky, and her mom jumped a little.

"Oops," said her mother. "You caught me."

"They're just fig newtons," said Becky. "They're low fat. And I think they have fiber."

Her mom chuckled.

"You're sweet," she said. "But you should be asleep."

"Yeah, about that. I kinda can't."

"What's the matter, hun?"

Becky sat down, sighed, and put her face in her hands.

"I can't believe I'm about to tell you this."

"Oh, Lord," said Becky's mom, the color draining from her face. "You're pregnant, aren't you?"

"Mom! No!"

"Well, you never know nowadays. Just the other day, Phyllis Henry told me that her niece . . ."

Becky had to stop this train before it left the station.

"Mom, I am not pregnant. But I still need to talk to you about something."

"Are you in some kind of trouble?"

"No, I don't think so."

"Rebecca, you are about to give me a heart attack. Just spit it out before I flip my lid."

"Okay," said Becky. "But I'm not entirely sure what happened or how to explain it."

Before she came into the kitchen, Becky wanted nothing more than to unburden herself of the guilt and confusion she felt. Now, she was pretty sure that trying to tell her mother about her first orgasm was the worst idea she'd ever had. She started with a vague account of what happened, hoping that her mother would catch on. She didn't. Instead, her mother just kept asking questions that forced Becky to be more and more specific.

At last, Becky blurted out, "I had an orgasm while Patrick and I were kissing!" Her head dropped to the kitchen table, and she buried it under her arms, awaiting death by humiliation.

Her mom sat in silence for a moment. Then she reached for another fig newton and took a bite. "But you guys weren't having sex, right?" she asked with her mouth full.

"No," said Becky from underneath her arms.

"You had clothes on, and you weren't touching each other's privates? Just kissing?"

"Clothes on and just kissing. No touching."

"Hmm. And the two of you have never done any more than kiss and cuddle? Really?"

Becky looked up, "I promise, mom. That's all."

Her mom leaned across the table and kissed Becky on the forehead.

"I am so proud of you. God blessed me with a daughter I hardly deserve."

Tears came to Becky's eyes, though she didn't know why.

"So, that was okay? We didn't do anything wrong?"

"No, you're fine. I mean, be careful. That kind of passion can get away from you. I wouldn't expect it to happen again, at least not very often. If you start trying to make it happen before you're married, it turns into a slippery slope. But no, sweetie, you didn't do anything wrong. You're just a teenage girl in love, and your body had a response to that. Nothing you could do about it."

Becky's shoulders dropped. She suddenly felt sleepy. She got up and gave her mother a hug.

"I love you, mom," she said. "Thanks so much for talking to me."

"Anytime, sweetie. I know it probably feels strange to talk to me about these things, but I'm glad you did. I want you to feel comfortable talking to me about anything."

"You definitely made me feel better," said Becky.

"Actually, you're really lucky," said her mother.

"What do you mean?"

"I wish it were that easy for me to have an orgasm."

Ew! thought Becky.

"Goodnight, mom! Gotta go to bed. School tomorrow," she said and vanished from the kitchen.

*****

Two months later, Brother Wayne asked Rebecca to stop by his office after school. He said it was about "leadership possibilities for the coming year." Rebecca wasn't surprised. Wayne had been after her to run for president of the youth group for a long time. Her answer had always been the same: She was too busy at school. Her answer would be the same this time, but she didn't want to be rude, so she agreed to meet with him.

Wayne asked if they could open in prayer. He prayed for God to guide their conversation, and Rebecca found it hard not to be cynical. She appreciated Wayne's teaching and guidance, but she knew his tactics. When she refused to run for youth group president, Wayne would respond with a not-so-subtle suggestion that she wasn't following God's will. Becky figured that if God wanted her to be youth group president, he would at least have put an inkling of desire in her heart and not rely only on Brother Wayne's pestering.

Wayne gave his usual argument. She had natural leadership skills. She was bright. She was godly. She was liked and respected. "I can tell that God really wants to use you, Rebecca," said Wayne. "All you need to do is respond."

"I'm not saying you're wrong," said Becky. "But maybe this isn't the time or even the place. I'm taking three AP classes next year. I'm president of the French Honor Society, and I'm thinking of trying out for tennis. I have a lot going on."

"And God's not more important than that?"

"Of course, not," said Becky. "I think there are more ways to serve God than being youth group president. Maybe I can serve God more by being a witness at school than a leader at church."

Wayne didn't have a rebuttal for that, so he just started at her with a feline grin. "You're under a lot of stress, aren't you?"

Finally, some empathy. "Yeah, you could say that," she said. "My plate is pretty full."

"I can tell that you're pretty tense all the time."

Becky shrugged. "I guess so, sure."

"Let me see if I can help," said Wayne.

He got up, walked around the desk, and stood behind her. When he put his hands on her shoulders, she jumped like someone had shocked her.

"Wow," said Wayne. "You really are tense." He started to massage her shoulders. The more he did it, the more her muscles tightened. "It's okay," he said. "Try to relax."

Relax was the last thing she could do. This was awful. She knew Wayne shouldn't be doing this. Then images of a hundred other little touches and caresses surfaced in her memory. Wayne had been touching her in odd ways since she was thirteen, but this was the first time he'd been so brazen about it.

Paralysis took hold. *Why can't I move? Why can't I say anything?*

"That's better," said Wayne.

Once his hands slid up from her shoulder and onto her neck. Then Becky felt his fingers creep up beneath her hair and start massaging her scalp. That fired her muscles back to life. She shot up so fast that one of Wayne's fingernails scratched her scalp.

"Hey, calm down!" said Wayne.

Becky ran out the door of his office and didn't stop until she got to her car. She drove straight to Patrick's house, bawling.

"What's wrong," he demanded, but she wouldn't tell him. He finally persuaded her to go Dairy Queen. She sat across from him in silence, picking at a parfait.

"I'm sorry," she said. "I know this must be hard for you, but I can't talk. I just need to go home. I just want to go to bed."

"It's 4:45 in the afternoon," said Patrick.

"It feels like midnight."

Patrick walked Becky to her car. He said he would be praying for her and leaned in to kiss her goodbye. She blocked him with a firm hand to his chest.

"No!"

"What? Why?"

"We're not doing that anymore."

"Not doing what?"

"Kissing or anything. It's wrong."

"Since when?"

"Since I said so. You need to respect me. You need to guard my heart. Or are your hormones more important than my heart?"

That was too much for Patrick. He had exercised far too much restraint to suffer such low blow. "If my hormones were more important," he said. "I would be dating someone else." He regretted saying it as soon as the words left his mouth.

"Screw you!" snapped Becky. She got in her car and slammed the door.

"Becky, stop! I'm sorry!" shouted Patrick, but she was gone.

*****

Becky didn't go to school the next day. She told her mother she was sick. Her mom knew better but didn't ask questions. She did start asking questions when Becky stopped going to youth group. She went to Sunday morning services and sat with her parents, but she refused to go to any youth group meetings. Becky was terrified to be in the same room with Brother Wayne, but she said she was quitting youth group because she and Patrick had broken up, and it was too painful to see him.

Only she hadn't broken up with Patrick, not officially. She just refused to return his texts, calls, and emails. She avoided him at school. At first, this just made Patrick angry, and he vowed to let her go if she was going to act like a crazy woman. But it didn't take long for him to go crazy himself. It was all he could do not to stalk her. He sent late night emails and texts. He left cards in her locker. He sent flowers. He would show up at her house. Usually, Becky's mother would show up with a lame excuse and a sympathetic look. Then, one day Becky's father showed up at the door.

When Patrick saw him, his stomach jumped up into his chest. A girl's father is an unwelcome sight when a boy is having trouble with his beloved.

"What's going on, Patrick?" said Becky's father. "You've been calling here a lot lately even though it seems that Rebecca doesn't want to talk to you."

Patrick took a deep breath. He knew that Becky's father had a gun, a very large gun, but it wasn't in sight. Nothing to lose.

"I'm sorry, sir," said Patrick. "But no one will give me any answers. Becky just stopped talking to me without telling me why. After a year and half together, I think I deserve to know what I did wrong."

Becky's father studied him for a moment.

"Is that the truth, son?"

"Yes, sir."

"You didn't do anything to hurt her?"

"Not that I know of, sir."

Becky's father paused.

"Well, come on in then."

Patrick followed Becky's father into the house, uncertain if he would come out alive. They walked to Becky's room. The door was closed. The muffled sound of Allison Krauss came from behind. Becky's father knocked.

"Come in," came the sound of Becky's voice.

Becky's father opened the door. "Rebecca, you have a visitor."

She was sitting on her bed surrounded by schoolwork. Her eyes widened when she saw Patrick.

"Daddy! What are you doing?"

"Something you should have done a long time ago. Put on some shoes and go sit on the porch with Patrick. You owe him an explanation. He can stay for dinner if he likes and if the two of you can be civil."

Becky's eyes narrowed. She threw a book on the bed, got up, and put on some sandals.

She rolled her eyes at Patrick and said, "Well, come on."

On the porch, Becky pouted for a few minutes. Patrick started by making small talk. Eventually, Becky joined in. In a few minutes, they were laughing. Becky had forgotten how good he could make her feel.

"I'm sorry, Patrick," she said. "I handled this whole thing wrong."

Patrick said nothing.

"I still can't tell you what happened. I haven't told anyone, but it has nothing to do with you. But, if we're going to be together, we can only be friends for now."

Patrick made a face like he'd swallowed vinegar.

"Sounds like a hoot," he said.

"I'm serious," she said. "If you mean all the things you said in those emails and cards, if you really love me, you'll be my friend for now."

Patrick folded his arms and put his head down.

"Okay," he said. "As long as we get to see each other again."

Becky patted his arm, "You bet, buddy."

"Do *not* call me 'buddy'!"

"Sorry," said Becky. "Overkill."

*****

Sexual trauma can lead to chronic fear. Fear activates the primitive parts of the brain that oversimplify everything. The world turns black and white. "A" always equals "B," and wherever there is smoke there will always be fire.

Most of the time, this is an adaptive cognitive feature. You'll live longer if you rule out the possibility of fire every time you smell smoke. Chronic fear resulting from trauma, however, is not adaptive; it's impairing. It's a psychological symptom that interferes with life.

Becky experienced sexual trauma at the hands of Brother Wayne, even though what he did to her wasn't explicitly sexual. It didn't have to be. Wayne was what psychoanalysts call a "powerful other" in Becky's life. He occupied a role of authority and wisdom. He was the authority on God and truth, a pillar of her morality. Wayne had become her inner compass for right and wrong, a source for validating her own goodness. When he tried to seduce her, her internal world collapsed. She became terrified, and her primitive brain went to work.

She reduced sexuality to a binary code. Romance, because it involved physical intimacy, was bad. Friendship, because it was free of physical intimacy, was good.

Psychologists call this "splitting," a reduction of people and relationships into all-good or all-bad propositions. Splitting frequently results from sexual trauma. Some trauma victims even split in way that makes promiscuous sex feel safe while emotional intimacy feels dangerous. Becky went the other direction. She made romance and physical intimacy bad. It's the only way she could cope with it. She also grew up in a culture that fully endorsed her primitive, unhealthy coping.

The Evangelical message to youth about sexuality sometimes makes the Church sound like a trauma victim. Here are some common Evangelical messages about love and romance for single folks:

Focus on the friendship, even when a relationship feels categorically different than any of your friendships.

Save kissing for the altar, because saving sex is for underachievers. And ignore all that kissing and touching in the Song of Songs, because the Song of Songs is really just a metaphor for Jesus. No, really, that's what someone told us.

Sexual desires are lustful and selfish, even though God created them and we need them to make more humans.

Men are lustful. Women are emotional. We call lustful women "whores." If a man shows a lot of emotion, he's probably gay.

Emotional intimacy has nothing to do with physical intimacy. God made Adam and Eve ghosts the first time around, but it spooked all the animals, so he threw some skin on them. Before you're married, God's only intention for your body is eating, sleeping, and processing waste. Keep your body away from others.

Okay, I might be using some hyperbole, maybe even sarcasm, but you get the point. These messages are based on fear. Maybe that's because so many Christians have been hurt in the process of looking for the right match and learning how to love and be loved. I can sympathize and empathize with that. We need help recovering from such wounds, and then we need to use them as opportunities for growth. What we cannot do is label love as dangerous just because some people get hurt.

After Pastor Wayne seduced Becky, love and intimacy felt dangerous. But since God created humans for love and intimacy, even the fear of danger couldn't keep her away from Patrick for long.

*****

Becky and Patrick were friends for three months, and they hated it. The only thing that was different from dating was that they didn't touch each other. They did things together, but they never did anything that felt too romantic. When they felt good about each other, they tried to put into words what only a hug or kiss could express. They loved each other but tried not to say so. If Patrick spent too much time with another girl, Becky got mad at Patrick but felt that it was wrong to tell him so. When Patrick asked when they could try dating again, Becky would always say, "soon," but the moment never came.

The incident with Wayne made her feel dirty. It made touching and anything to do with bodies and sex and men feel wrong. Intellectually, she knew that she had done nothing wrong, but she couldn't shake the feeling that it was somehow her fault. Ever since she was twelve, she had learned that women should be careful about tempting men with their bodies. They should dress modestly and avoid making men "stumble." Becky didn't dress provocatively, but she liked to look pretty. She knew which clothes made her look cute. She knew which outfits Patrick liked without him saying so. Looking good made her feel good.

Though she was furious with Brother Wayne, a part of her wondered if she hadn't been at fault. Ever since the back-rub incident, Becky had stopped wearing make-up. She went out of her way to dress in unflattering clothes. It got so bad that her father sent her off to school one morning by saying, "Have a nice day, bag lady." Still, Patrick never complained. He remained her "friend" and said nothing about her fashion downgrade.

On a muggy evening in August, Patrick dropped by Becky's house with a couple of videos. Since they never went on real "dates," they spent a lot of time watching movies at Becky's house while her parents were home.

As they were about to start up the movie, Becky's mom and dad came into the room. "We need to talk to you two," said Becky's father. He sat down in his recliner. Becky's mom sat down next to Becky and grabbed her hand

"This news is going to be shocking," said Becky's father. "So I'm going to tell you, and then I want us to talk about it. Then I think we should have a time of prayer."

"What happened?" asked Becky.

"Well, it turns out that Brother Wayne has been having inappropriate relationships with some girls at the church. One girl got pregnant and told her parents, who told Pastor Newton. Then two other girls came forward and said that Brother Wayne had seduced them into sexual relationships, as well. He's been fired and brought up on criminal charges for statutory rape."

Patrick and Becky looked at each other. Becky's eyes filled with tears.

"I'm so sorry," Patrick said to Becky. "I never knew something like this would upset you so much."

"Aren't you upset?" asked Becky.

"I guess so," said Patrick. "I don't know. I always thought Wayne was kind of a tool. This is shocking but not terribly surprising, if you know what I mean."

Becky understood more than he knew. She wasn't crying tears of sadness. She wasn't sure why she was crying. It wasn't quite relief. Was it vindication? No, it was anger, simple rage. Wayne and everything he taught had been a lie. A terrible, hypocritical lie from a sexual deviant. She had not been too cute or too sexy. In fact, she realized that she had no idea how she felt about her own sexuality. She had learned about sexual morality from a pervert, so what was she supposed to believe?

Becky's parents talked with them for a few more minutes. Then her father led them in prayer. But Becky wasn't praying; she was plotting. After her father finished praying, everyone hugged. Becky hugged Patrick a little harder and longer than usual, pressing her chest into him.

"Mom and dad," said Becky. "Are you guys in the mood for Chinese food at all?"

"Now you're talking, young lady!" said her father.

"Well," said Becky. "I was thinking that y'all could go pick some up while we get started on the movie, so Patrick isn't here too late. Or I guess we could get some if you don't feel like going out."

It would be better if her parents left, but her plan would work as long as she and Patrick were alone.

"We could all go," said her mother.

Becky was prepared for such a response. "Don't take this the wrong way," she said. "But I kind of want to talk all this over with Patrick alone for a while. There are some things I need to share with him in private."

Her parents looked at each other and smiled. "I'll tell you what," said her father. "If y'all aren't too hungry, your mother and I will go eat at the restaurant. We'll take our time. Then we'll bring y'all back whatever you want. How does that sound?"

Perfect answer, thought Becky.

"Are you sure you don't mind?" asked Patrick.

"No, that's fine," said Becky's mother. "Just tell us what you want to eat."

Becky's parents took down their orders, refusing Patrick's offers to chip in some money. Then they left. Becky knew they would be gone for over an hour.

When their car pulled out of the driveway, Becky grabbed Patrick's hand. "Follow me," she said and pulled him off the couch.

She dragged him into her bedroom, closed the door, and locked it, just in case. "Take off your clothes," she said.

Patrick's eyes popped open, and his head went back.

"Um, why?"

"Because I'm taking off mine, and this won't be as much fun if I'm the only one who is naked."

*****

Without wholeness, we go to extremes. Rigidity and legalism don't always favor restraint. The primitive parts of our brains can make just as much use of black-and-white thinking for self-indulgence.

When Becky dragged Patrick into the bedroom, it might seem like she was indulging in lust, but her motivation was more complicated and more troubling than simple lust. She was angry. More than that, she was reasserting dominance, not over Patrick, but over herself. When Pastor Wayne seduced her, he shook the foundation of her morality and frightened her away from intimacy. When she had confirmation that she was just one of many victims and did nothing to provoke him, she wanted to feel in control again.

The problem is that Becky had no idea what empowerment looked and felt like when it came to sexuality for a single, Christian young woman. She knew it meant abstinence. She had gone beyond abstinence to total restraint. It helped her feel in control, but she hated it.

When she learned about Pastor Wayne's abuse of other girls in the church, her anger made her feel out of control again. She was furious that she had rejected intimacy because of a sexual predator. But she had no model of intimacy for single Christians. She rejected the model of restraint given to her by the sexual deviant posing as her youth pastor, but she didn't know how to recover and restore her own healthy, holy sexuality.

With no other options, she went to the opposite extreme. Well, almost.

*****

Patrick and Becky didn't have sex, at least not sexual intercourse. In the following months, they explored each other's bodies with abandon. Each time they halted breathlessly before reaching oral sex or intercourse. They never discussed it, but almost every time they were alone clothes came off. They felt guilty sometimes but never talked about it. The only thing they talked about was how incredible it would be to finally go all the way once they were married.

Becky and Patrick got married the summer between their sophomore and junior year of college. The wedding was beautiful, a celebration filled with friends, family, and love. The happy couple left the reception early, abandoning their loved ones to a DJ whose music collection hadn't been updated since the late nineties.

Patrick whisked Becky over the threshold of their honeymoon suite, and they began tearing off clothes. Then they pounced on the bed and commenced the attack.

It began with affection and passion. The first few awkward stumbles didn't dampen the mood. Then more obstacles arose until the moment they had fantasized about became an embarrassing puzzle. Once they solved the puzzle, they discovered, to their horror, that it was painful, but mostly for Becky. They finished and rolled away from each other, not knowing what to say.

"We're just tired," said Patrick. "The honeymoon will be better."

That made Becky feel better. She nuzzled into Patrick and fell asleep.

But things didn't get better, not during the honeymoon, and not during their first year of marriage. Sex felt like work. It was a problem that they couldn't solve. As a result, they began to avoid it. Gone was the passion they felt for each other every moment until they said their vows. The situation deteriorated into acrimony and resentment. After months of giving each other no more than a polite peck on a cheek, Becky asked her best friend for a referral for couples therapy.

*****

After Becky and Patrick told me about Wayne's statutory rape of the girls he was supposed to guide and protect, something clicked.

"I wouldn't expect you guys to have a good sex life after marriage. In fact, it was almost impossible."

Becky sighed and looked down.

"It's because we fooled around too much while were dating," she said. "I always heard that it could ruin sex once you're married."

"Nope," I said. "That's not it."

Becky looked surprised. Patrick said, "cool," and Becky gave him a dirty look. Then she turned it on me.

"You mean that you think everything we did before marriage was okay?"

"I don't know," I said. "It sounds like you did some of it out of anger. It sounds like maybe you didn't think all of it through. Maybe you could have been more careful. But there's nothing in the Bible and nothing in the sexuality research that indicates that you somehow screwed up your sex life."

"So what's the matter?" said Patrick.

"Marriage is holy. Marriage is sacred. But the only message you got about sexuality is that it's dirty. Think about it: You got all these negative messages from all of these adults when you were kids. Patrick, your mom made you feel rotten about your sexuality. She said you would be better off being a crackhead! I think even the crackheads would disagree with that. Becky, you felt like your sexuality was responsible for someone else's sin. Then, to make matters worse, the main Christian leader in your life is disgraced and even gets arrested because of his sexual behavior. The only thing you learned about sexuality is that it's damaging and harmful. How does something like that have a place in marriage?"

"It's weird," said Patrick. "Sex just felt a lot . . . *sexier* before we were married."

I nodded my head. It was something I heard all the time.

"That's because it felt forbidden, like something dangerous. That's the only way you understood it. You guys can't see it as having a place in something holy like marriage because of all the damage that's been done. You might have made some mistakes, but you were set up for this in a lot of ways. No one taught you how to think about sexuality and God as going together."

"What do we do?" asked Becky. "What's next?"

"There are a lot of things you can do. That's the good news. Some of them are simple things you can try tonight if you want to. But the hardest part will be making sexuality feel like something good, like something God created."

Becky sighed, "Honestly, I know you're right, but that feels impossible."

"I totally get that," I said. "But it's not impossible. It will be hard, but not as hard as you think."

"Well," said Patrick, "I think it will be easier with your help."

"I'm going to do my best," I said. "But I'm just a psychologist who knows some things about sex. I didn't *create* sex. Fortunately, you guys know the One who did."

"Amen," said Becky. "I really want to start thinking that way. I want to see God as part of our sex lives. That way, I think this won't be so hard."

"Oh, it's going to be *hard*, all right," said Patrick.

My hand shot up and covered my mouth.

"Oh, honey," said Becky. "That makes me sad. What makes you think it will be hard?"

She saw his wicked grin and the mischievous look in his eye.

"You are such a punk!" she shouted and socked him in the arm.

Patrick doubled over laughing. Becky rolled her eyes but started to laugh. Patrick swallowed her in a hug and whisked her out the door.

As I watched them go, I started laughing, too. I was laughing at Patrick's naughty joke, and I was laughing over the joy of rebirth and God's grace.

Chapter Five:
Brian

At the beginning, I told you that everything in this book is "true but not real." I changed a lot of things in order to hide identifying information and give myself some creative wiggle room. Strictly speaking, the stories in this book are all fictional.

Except for this one.

My friend "Brian" encouraged me to tell his real story in the hope that it would help others. Though I would have been happy to make changes in order to protect Brian's privacy, his story doesn't need any creative enhancement. It's powerful enough on its own. I insisted on changing only his name, despite the fact that he gave me permission to use his real one. Brian has always been fearless. Well, he always seemed that way to me. I came to find out that that Brian has lived much of his life in fear and confusion.

I'm not going to tell Brian's story from his point of view, like I have the others. I'm going to tell it from mine, instead. I watched some of Brian's story from the cheap seats. Then we lost touch for twenty years. We reconnected one December at his home in New York City. After a long night of fun, he began filling in the missing pieces. What he shared left me astonished, grateful, and ashamed.

*****

If you're a night owl like me, it feels like God made New York City just for you. If you share my unhealthy attachment to rich, savory food, then it can feel like heaven. I doubt that New York is most people's idea of heaven. Honestly, it's not really mine. I live in Los Angeles, after all, and the novelty of cold weather expires after about forty-eight hours. But, walking down Amsterdam Avenue at 9:45 p.m. on a Saturday just before Christmas, the only thing missing was my wife on my arm. The night was bright and brisk but not too cold. One of the best cheeseburgers I'd ever tasted, courtesy of the Amsterdam Ale house, still lounged in my belly. I had a long walk ahead to let my dinner settle as I absorbed the quiet winter nocturne of the Upper West Side.

As I approached my destination, the sedating combo of comfort food and Sierra Nevada Pale Ale gave way to a touch of anxiety. I hadn't seen Brian in twenty years. Seeing someone after so much time would be a little weird for anyone. Meeting Brian at his own Christmas party packed with his own friends could make it more awkward. I didn't want to monopolize the host, but that meant socializing with strangers. I'm not bad at mixing with people I don't know, but I seldom do it by choice.

As I reached 90th Avenue, I forced myself to be honest about the real reason I was nervous: It was a safe bet that the majority of people at Brian's Christmas party would be gay, just like him. I didn't suffer from some homophobic paranoia about getting jumped by a bunch of gay guys. I'm a member of the Society for the Scientific Study of Sexuality, and I couldn't survive their annual meetings if sexual diversity made me nervous. I also had longtime gay friends.

One time my wife said to me, "Except for Mark and Jonathan, it seems like almost everyone you still know from college came out as gay."

I said, "No, that's not . . . yeah, kinda."

As a result, I knew that gay people are not rude to straight people. Moreover, Brian was the kind of guy to throw fun, classy parties. I wasn't scared, but I would be in the minority as a straight guy. I would feel out of place, like a Catholic visiting a Pentecostal church.

"Well," I whispered, my breath turning into steam. "I'll just have to suck it up. Brian has been through much worse." I said that based on what I knew at the time. I had no idea how much worse things had really been for Brian.

*****

Brian was my fraternity brother at Wake Forest University. Brian and I were friends, but Brian is many things that I am not. First, he likes people. I like people, too, but I have to get over being grouchy and cynical, and it takes me longer to warm up. That was never the case with Brian. He was friendly, but not in the superficially polite way one expects from southerners. His warmth feels genuine, not just nice. He's got a playful, slightly wicked sense of humor that helps people drop their guard.

Brian was also a leader. I'm a leader, too, but it usually happens because I can only stomach chaos for so long before I get off my ass and take the reins. Brian, on the other hand, wants things to change for the better. He has ambition, but it doesn't come across as selfish. He was instrumental in eliminating some vile hazing practices from our fraternity long after he'd already endured them.

And Brian is ridiculously smart. I'm smart, too, but it's on a selective basis and I turn off my brain and check out sometimes. Brian has a nuclear-powered brain. It moves fast. He comes up with witty anecdotes like Garrison Keillor on speed, and metaphors fly out of his mouth like Bernard Malamud on cocaine. If he had written this book, it would sell more copies, and you would have finished the whole thing in one sitting.

Brian was popular in my fraternity and popular on campus. I wasn't part of Brian's inner circle, but we spent quality time together in college. We went on road trips and came back with good stories. I could confide in him. We weren't best friends, but I felt lucky to count him as any kind of friend.

*****

"What you and nobody else knew at the time" said Brian as we sat on the fire escape in the alley behind his apartment, "was that I was sneaking away to hook up with a male law student in the parking lot of the football stadium."

What he said didn't shock me; I'm a psychologist. I've heard many stories in therapy about people struggling with secret homosexual feelings, and almost all of them include some type of clandestine sex. And Brian wasn't trying to shock me. He told me this to emphasize the juxtaposition between his public persona and the life he led in secret.

The party had been more fun than I expected. The apartment Brian shared with his partner looked great, and it was big, even by non-Manhattan standards. I knew that Brian was successful, but one look at his home told me that I had underestimated his accomplishments. The place was packed when I arrived, but Brian spotted me right away. He welcomed me with laughter and a big hug.

"You look exactly the same!" he said.

"You mean I've always looked like crap?" I said, and he laughed.

He took my coat and introduced me around. He even allowed me to tell embarrassing stories about him from college. His subordinates from work got a big kick out of that and threatened to spread them around the office. Eventually, he pointed me toward the food and drinks, promising to find me later. I got a drink and a plate of food, then found a seat near a group of people that looked to be about my age. They were talking loudly and laughing. At the first lull in the conversation, they all looked at me at once.

"Hi. I'm Steve from LA. I don't know anyone."

The life drained out of their conversation as if I'd told them I had the Ebola virus. But I had a secret weapon, one that never failed me in the small-talk arena. "My wife and I have seven-year-old quadruplets," I said. "All natural, no in-vitro. Three girls and a boy."

Gasps. Accusations of dishonesty. Requests for pictures. Questions. Laughter. Five minutes later I have new friends based solely on the merits of my wife and children. Between my kids and college stories about Brian, I knew everyone at the party by midnight.

People started to trickle out around one a.m. That's when Brian found me spearing meatballs out of a crockpot with toothpicks.

He handed me a glass of wine and said, "I don't care if it takes until dawn, we are making up for lost time."

It was the first time we had really talked since he came out as gay in the mid-nineties. I was interested in his story, but I didn't want to push a sensitive topic. I didn't have to.

"I think it's important that we talk about it, that you know everything that happened," he said. "When I first came out, I was so angry. All these people I thought were so close to me in college just backed away. So I was like, 'Fine, I'm breaking ties with everyone.' College was such a painful time and so few of my straight friends were supportive, I just didn't give anyone a chance."

"Wow," I said. "You seemed to have everything so together in college. I had no idea things were so bad for you."

Brian rolled his eyes. "I was leading two different lives."

This is something I hear a lot from homosexuals "in the closet." They confine the homosexual side of their identity to secret places. Dark places, where the light of reason and support of community aren't available. Their sexuality splits off from the rest of who they are. This doesn't excuse the mistakes, but it's easy to understand how it makes them vulnerable to impulsive, secretive hook ups. If you can never think or talk about your sexuality, it sneaks up on you.

Brian was trying to live a Christian life, though the torment he felt over his homosexuality made that feel less possible as time went on. Brian did his best to lead a straight life. He begged God to remove his feelings of homosexuality. He was active in Christian groups on campus and in the fraternity Bible study. He had a long-term relationship with a sweet girl that everyone liked. Then, one day, they inexplicably broke up.

"I was devastated when she broke up with me. I really cared about her, but she was sexually frustrated."

I asked Brian if he meant she wanted to have sex.

"No," he said. "But she could tell there was something missing in the physical dimension of our relationship. We weren't connecting physically like we should have. The physical intimacy, the affection wasn't there, and I think she took it personally. I wish I could have told her the real reason, though I'm not sure she would have taken it any better."

Brian began his stealth relationship with the law student during his junior year. They were both in the closet, so they confined their encounters to trysts in secret places, like the football field parking lot.

"Can you imagine how people in our fraternity would have reacted if they had known that was going on?"

"Yes," I said. "It would have been ugly."

"So you can see why I didn't exactly feel safe to come out."

"Of course, I understand, dude," I said. "But you had another chance to talk to me. What happened there? I would have been there for you."

Brian took a slow sip of his wine and stared at the building looming across from us in the darkness. "I believe you," he said. "But you have to understand I was still leading two lives, even when we were in D.C."

*****

The year after I graduated from college was one of the worst times of my life. One of my lifelong best friends died. My girlfriend of three years dumped me right after I moved to Washington D.C. in order to live closer to her. I never had enough money. My car broke down all the time. My first real job as a youth pastor for a mainline denominational church started well, but it soon became clear that even my centrist, inclusive version of Evangelical Christianity was too conservative for them. I got a crush on the church secretary's daughter, who kept me on the line for a few weeks before telling me she had a boyfriend. The only tolerable time during my first year out of college was when Brian slept on my floor for three months.

Brian called in September of 1991. He'd taken a job at a private school in Georgia, though that seemed a little lackluster for Brian. I guess it was because he was an English major, and they don't exactly hurl high profile jobs at English majors right out of school. Regardless,

Brian didn't last long and got the urge to work in politics or, as he was always quick to correct me, "statesmanship." With typical Brian gusto, he planned to move to D.C. with no job and no prospects. He asked if he could crash on my floor and chip in with rent while he looked for a job as a staffer on Capitol Hill. I was delighted. I even vacuumed the spot where he would be sleeping.

Having Brian live with me was a blessing. I didn't know anyone in D.C. other than my sister and my girlfriend, and she was away at college. Finally, I had a male friend my age in town, living in my apartment no less. Brian and I went running together. We explored the city together. We checked out the nightlife. Brian was my biggest supporter as I worked through the breakup with my girlfriend. Life would have been miserable without him.

Brian was even an asset to my youth ministry. Any youth pastor will tell you that you're always eager for good volunteers, and Brian had more instinctive youth ministry skills than I did. His time around the church was short-lived, but the kids loved him. He had great insights about Scripture and surviving the trials and tribulations of adolescence.

One of the fun things about Brian living with me while he explored a career in politics was that he was a Republican and I am not. Cool your jets, I'm pro-life and I'm just left of center, so it's not a big deal. That's not the point. The point is that I express affection through playful taunting and teasing. I'm not proud of it, and I don't encourage it in others, but I can't help myself. Someone with career aspirations in the Republican party sleeping on the floor made for plenty of good-natured verbal jousting.

Before long, however, I didn't have the heart to give Brian a hard time about politics. He had left a steady job to chase his dreams, so I tried to be supportive. We had spirited debates from time to time, but I kept the teasing about politics to a minimum. I soon found two other opportunities for mischief.

First, I discovered that Brian has a potent startle reflex. I was renting a basement, and a sliding glass door was the primary entrance. We accessed the sliding glass door by taking a short path through a thicket of trees near the street. At night, the dense line of trees at the back of the house made the view from the sliding glass door dark and spooky.

Since I had meetings almost every night at church, I usually arrived home after Brian. I would creep up the path and spy Brian cozied up on his air mattress in the middle of floor, watching television or reading. I could see him, but he couldn't see me behind the glare of the sliding glass door. I would wait until I knew Brian hadn't spotted me and then pound my knuckles on the glass in rapid-fire succession. *Rat-tat-tat-tat-tat-tat-tat-tat!*

Brian's whole body would convulse. Some nights he would jump clear off his mattress. Then he would shoot me a hostile scowl as I doubled over laughing. "You . . . are . . . an asshole!" he would shout, or some variation.

"What did I do?" I would say, still laughing as I opened the door.

"You know exactly what you did!"

"You're right."

The most remarkable thing about this was that it worked every time.

The second thing that I discovered was that Brian had become a big homophobe since we graduated college. He had not come out yet, and I had no inclination that Brian might be gay. I assumed his homophobia was a distasteful outgrowth of his conservative ways. And I decided to have as much fun with it as possible.

We went to Georgetown on Halloween night. We had heard that it was a little wild and everyone packed the streets wearing costumes. I arrived home from a Halloween party at church around nine p.m. I was dressed like a zombie in a trench coat. I had on ghoulish white make up, complete with makeshift lesions and sores created from fake blood.

"Brian!" I called. "Are you ready?"

"I'm upstairs with Vickie," he said. Vickie was my landlady, a single mom who lived on the stop floor. "Come up here and tell me how I look."

I hopped up the stairs. When I saw Brian, I bit my lip, stifling a laugh.

"Now, be honest, Steve. Tell me the truth. Do I look like a fag?"

Brian had on black running rights. Over those, he wore a colorful court jester outfit, complete with a floppy hat with bells on it. The costume had obviously been designed for a woman.

"I borrowed this from Vickie," said Brian.

Never would have guessed.

"Be honest, Steve. Do I look like a fag?"

In my mind, a mischievous grin spread from ear to ear.

"Don't worry," I said. "You look fine."

We took the Metro down to Georgetown. The whole time, Brian kept saying, "People are going to think we're gay, people are going to think we're gay." I reassured him that wasn't the case. Then I stopped reassuring him and started trying to hold his hand.

Every time I reached down and grabbed Brian's hand, he jumped as if I had zapped him with a thousand volts. After a while, he got wise and kept his distance. Then he would forget, and I'd do it again. Brian laughed a little every time, so I didn't feel too sadistic.

We made our way through Georgetown, unimpressed with the spectacle. It was mostly just crowded and hard to walk. As we made our way back toward the Metro, I saw group of guys ahead, sitting on a wall. They were heckling people who passed by.

This is going to be bad.

I looked for an alternate route, but the streets were crowded, and we had to move with the herd. We were almost past them when one of them spied Brian.

"Hey, are you supposed to be a court jester or something?"

"Yes, sir," said Brian. "That's exactly right."

"You look more like a faggot!" All the guys on the wall burst out in laughter.

I admit that I started to chuckle. I thought that Brian was not only heterosexual, but homophobic, which made it especially funny. It was comic justice.

"Stop it!" shouted Brian.

"What?" I said.

"Stop laughing. You said I didn't look like a fag, and I obviously do."

I felt bad and tried to backpedal.

"Hey, man, I'm sorry. I was just messing around. Don't take it –"

"Shut up, Steve. You play around too much."

That stung. I shut my mouth and gave him some space.

Brian was quiet most of the way home. It wasn't the first time I had pushed a joke too far and hurt someone's feelings. This was more evidence I still had work to do in this area. Still, I didn't understand why Brian was so angry. Was he really that homophobic?

*****

"I wasn't homophobic, I was homosexual," said Brian, laughing as I recounted the story. "Homophobia was my last gasp effort at hiding it. Everything came to a head when I was in D.C. I was more confused and miserable than ever."

"I'm so sorry about that stunt," I said. "I never would have done that had I known. I guess my gay-dar wasn't very good. That must have been awful for you."

"You don't have to apologize," said Brian. "It would have been a lot funnier if there hadn't been so many confusing things going on at the time. There was a lot happening while I was sleeping on your floor that you didn't know about."

"Like what?"

Brian sighed. His breath turned to steam in the December air. He looked at his watch.

"Do you realize it's almost four a.m.?"

"Seriously?"

We had been talking for three hours. It felt like thirty minutes.

"Guess it's time to wrap it up," I said. "But I want us to keep talking."

"Absolutely. Let's make sure that happens."

Brian walked me out to the street. He lived in a quiet part of Manhattan where cabs were scarce at four in the morning. Brian waited with me as we watched for signs of anything yellow.

"I'm working on a book about sexuality for unmarried Christians," I told him. "I think it might be good to include your story. Do you think we could talk more, and maybe I could write something about you?"

Brian didn't hesitate.

"I would be honored, and I will tell you anything you want to know."

A cab appeared out of the darkness and we waved it down.

"We are *not* letting another twenty years go by before we do this again," I said.

"No way, brother," Brian said.

We hugged goodbye, and I got into the cab. Brian told the driver where to go.

I watched buildings pass for a few blocks. Then I leaned back in the seat and closed my eyes.

"Thank you for that, Lord," I whispered.

*****

On a perfect Los Angeles day in May, I sat down at my kitchen table, popped open my computer, and called Brian at his office in New York. Since Brian travels the world for weeks at a time, we had scheduled this call far in advance. Check Brian's Facebook page on any given day and you're just as likely to find him in Asia or Europe as New York City. Sometimes Brian will even turn up in LA, but I know better than to try to get together with him. He'll be scheduled wall-to-wall. I didn't take it for granted that he was making time to help out with my book.

I called Brian's assistant, and she asked me to wait for a minute or two. Then Brian's voice came on the line. We joked around for a few minutes before jumping into his story.

"I see you traveling around the world everywhere on your Facebook page," I said. "You're like a first-class hobo."

"I'm a first-class hobo homo," he said.

"Nice segue," I said. "Where do you want to start?"

"The beginning."

*****

Brian grew up in a family that was more conservative than religious. Being Southern Baptist was part of being conservative, not vice versa. Brian stepped up his involvement in church mainly as a way to combat his homosexual feelings.

"I had always felt like there was something different about me, but it became obvious in adolescence. The message I'd always received was that homosexuality was a perversion, something evil. Whether it was my father's gay jokes or my pastor calling homosexuality an abomination, I knew that I was flawed. So I ran to God and the church to fix me.

"I became more involved in church. I became a leader. I started meeting with my pastor for one-on-one Bible study in the morning before school. I prayed and prayed for God to take away my homosexual feelings, but it didn't happen. Whenever I went to church and left still feeling gay I would think, 'Well, God didn't show up today.'

"Some days I would leave church and go to the mall to meet other guys. They would be gay but in the closet like me. It's not like anyone was out in my town. We would find a secret place to make out or fool around a little. Then I would go back to feeling guilty and terrible about myself again, begging God for forgiveness and begging God to make it stop."

Brian struggled with homosexual feelings and hated himself for it throughout high school and into college. I can vouch for the fact that he did a great job of keeping his homosexuality a secret. Brian never had difficulty making friends with heterosexual, masculine guys. In our fraternity, he was friends with all the popular athletes, guys that were *very* heterosexual and had no trouble with the ladies. I asked Brian what it was like being so close to so many straight guys.

"I lived in constant fear of being discovered. I worried that I might drink too much one night and say or do something that would give away my secret. It made my life miserable. I thought about ways to commit suicide. In high school, I thought about shooting myself sometimes. In college, I would imagine driving my car off the road, over a cliff, or speeding into a wall. It was miserable to be so close to these people who would reject you if they knew the truth."

Despite all this, Brian hadn't walked away from his faith. He still asked God to change him. He stayed active in campus ministry organizations. All that changed during Brian's sophomore year.

While Brian was pledging our fraternity, one of the brother's called and asked Brian to pick him up and drive him home from a bar. Brian didn't think anything of it at the time. Pledges were at the beck and call of the brothers, and it wasn't unusual for a brother who'd had too much to drink to call a pledge for a ride.

Brian picked up the brother and drove him home. The brother insisted that Brian come inside for a drink. Once they were inside, the brother began to seduce him. Conflicting feelings overwhelmed Brian, the same sort that I imagine confront others in his situation. Part of him felt like he couldn't give in to something wrong. However, another part of him, suppressed for so long, hiding in the dark, finally had the chance to be free. For closeted homosexuals, situations like this are far more complicated than the garden-variety sexual temptation that heterosexuals encounter. It's not just about lust. For a little while, they get to be who they really are. They get the freedom heterosexuals enjoy all the time. Though it's not an excuse, such temptation is difficult to resist.

Brian succumbed and had sex with the brother, assuming that it would remain a secret. What happened next, however, shocked Brian (and infuriated me when he told me).

The older fraternity brother told Brian's roommate, a devout Christian, what had happened. The brother framed it in terms of Brian failing in his faith and making a mistake. The brother took no responsibility at all, telling Brian's roommate that he was worried about Brian.

Brian returned to his room one night and found his roommate waiting for him.

"We need to talk," he said.

He confronted Brian about what happened. He said that something like this could never happen again, and he was going to hold Brian accountable. He made it clear that there was no place for homosexuality in the Christian faith. He told Brian that he needed to get right with God.

"That's when I decided that religion was not for me," Brian told me. "It's not that I stopped believing in God, but I couldn't handle the hypocrisy, especially after someone seduced me into having sex and then told my roommate about it because he was supposedly worried about my faith. That's insane. I couldn't handle it anymore. So, the next year, I moved into a single room in the dorm. I thought it was time for me to start handling things by myself."

Brian moved to D.C. the year after graduating college. Looking back, those few months that he slept on my floor were the best time I had living in D.C. I didn't know things were much harder for him, and about to get worse.

Moving to the big city exposed Brian to a new level of diversity and opportunity to explore his sexual orientation. He got hit on constantly by other men while working on Capitol Hill for a Republican congressman. Nevertheless, he refused to embrace his homosexuality. While he was going out to gay clubs in secret, he was still going out to straight clubs with me, playing the part of wingman as we tried to meet girls. He became active in a Methodist church. He met a woman and began dating her. She would be the last woman he would ever date.

Brian could no longer stomach hiding who he was. He knew that he was gay and would never be straight. Hours of praying and struggling had done nothing. He decided that it was time to accept who he was and get on with his life. The first step would be the hardest: telling his parents.

He had tried to tell them before, when he was younger. Their denial had been so thick and intense that it convinced even him that this was "just a phase." He knew that he had to stand his ground this time. He had to tell them that there would be no counseling to try to fix him. This was not a phase, and there was no going back. He expected the worst. He was right.

His parents had an emotional meltdown. They bargained. They pleaded. They tried to convince him to change and seek help. When Brian refused, they exiled him. They took his car away and drove him to the train station.

As he stood on the barren platform waiting for the train to arrive, the realization of how alone he was hit in crushing waves. He had just lost his family. Most of his friends had no idea he was gay. He knew that they would reject him when they found out. He felt God had abandoned him. Once he boarded that train, it would take him to a terrifying existence he would face alone.

Brian got on the train, and it took him to a new life. Ever since, he has faced life mostly by himself. That's the happy and sad end of this story.

Brian was angry for a long time. He was angry at his family, angry at his straight friends, and angry at God. It's a normal developmental stage for someone who has had to hide their sexual orientation for years. However, he gradually began reaching out to people, one by one. Sometimes he found acceptance and sometimes he didn't. Other people just faded out of his life. But he met new people. Brian has always made friends easily. He had romantic relationships, real ones, out in the open. Finally, in his thirties he entered a committed union with someone, and they settled down together in New York City.

Brian suffered a lot to get to the place he is now, but you would never know it by looking at his career. His achievements are staggering. He has been successful at most everything he's done. He's rich. He would say he's not, but living in New York City has impaired his cognitive ability to assess normal standards of living.

When I saw Brian for the first time in almost twenty years, it filled me with joy to see him happy, successful, and wealthy after going through so many years of pain. When I talked to him in May, however, he told me something that broke my heart.

"One last question," I said as our conversation came to a close. "You've been on quite the journey. What have you learned from it?"

Brian didn't hesitate. "No one will take care of me but me," he said. "There is no unconditional love between people."

Brian did not say it in anger. He did not say it in self-pity. He said it with gratitude. He said it as if he had learned a crucial, universal truth. His tone was cheerful.

Meanwhile, tears welled up in my eyes.

"I am so sorry," I said. "That's a horrible lesson to learn."

Brian paused for a moment, then said, "Oh, I think I see what you mean. But, man, you have to understand that I needed to think that way to survive. *It saved my life.*"

I asked if he felt like he had people he could count on now, people who loved him and would take care of him. He reassured me that he did, but it had nothing to do with church.

"I finally found peace by embracing that I was one of God's creations," Brian told me. "I don't really have space and place for religion, and I don't know that I ever will. Maybe I'm scapegoating religion. I don't know."

The other stories I've told you have happy endings. This one does too, but it doesn't resolve very well for Christians. Nobody in the Church helped Brian. If anything, Christians made things worse. We failed him. I failed him.

I knew he had come out as gay long before I finally saw him again at his Christmas party. I had known since the mid-nineties. I made some half-hearted attempts to reach him, but I could have done more. I should have done more. Brian gave me the respite I needed during one of the most difficult years of my life. He was fun, kind, patient, and generous. When I heard that he had come out as gay, I knew his life would explode and it would take years to pick up the pieces. I had a responsibility to do more, but I didn't.

This is Brian's success story, but it is not ours. The Church has failed the gay community. It would be easy to lapse into a discussion of theology about homosexuality, but that's not the point of this story. Regardless of our theological positions, we have failed. Too many people have suffered because we have been too selfish, too uncomfortable, or just too stubborn to show God's love to someone who seems different.

Proverbs 17:17 says, "A friend loves at all times, and a brother is born for adversity" (New International Version, NIV). We have not obeyed God. I have not obeyed God. I have failed, and Brian isn't the only one I've failed.

When I was sixteen, I was walking back from the baseball field with a bunch of other guys at the end of gym class. We were cutting up and laughing after playing softball on an immaculate Kentucky spring day. Everyone was in a good mood until a guy named Weasel ruined it.

"Hey, Eric, you suck dick, don't you?"

Weasel humiliated people for sport. His target today was Eric, the first gay person I ever knew.

"I don't see how you can suck dick. That's gross. C'mon, Eric, tell us how you do it."

Eric walked a few feet away from everyone else. He had a diminutive build and stood just over five feet tall. Eric fixed his eyes on the ground and quickened his pace. Weasel sped up and fell in behind him.

"It's a simple question," said Weasel. "I'd think a fag would know the answer."

I told myself that Eric could escape from Weasel if things got worse. Eric was fast. I knew this because we had been friends as children. We played together at recess and went to Cub Scouts together. He was the only one in fifth grade who could run faster than me. He had never bragged about it or taunted me. I just always came in second.

That awful day in high school gym class, I did not act like someone who had once been Eric's friend. I didn't stand up for him, but it wasn't because I was afraid of Weasel. I was a varsity wrestler, stronger and quicker than he was. I could have put Weasel down in two moves, and he never would have landed a punch. Still, I did nothing because I was afraid of being known as the guy who stood up for the fag. I didn't want people to think I was gay too. I was a selfish coward. I was a sinner.

I'm sorry, Eric. I'm sorry, Brian. I repent, and I want to do better. I pray that the Church can do better. We've failed, and we need to make it up to you.

When I asked Brian what Christians could have done differently as he struggled with his sexual orientation, this is what he told me:

"I don't think that Christianity and close-mindedness should be synonyms. There's no 'community' in Christianity, at least not in the way I define it. I didn't find community." He paused. "They could have loved me unconditionally."

Brian was a good friend, even when I played pranks on him and wasn't a very good friend in return. After he came out, I waited twenty years to reach out to him. I'm an asshole.

If the Body of Christ can't agree about theology when it comes to homosexuality, maybe we can at least agree not to be assholes. That's not enough, but it's a place to start.

Chapter Six:
Logan, Eliot, & Brian

A local Bible college sends me a lot of their "sex problem" referrals. Like most college counseling centers, they have fallen prey to the "ten-session maximum" rule perpetuated by insurance companies. In the school's defense, a lot of students come to them for help, and they have to limit the number of sessions in order to see as many people as possible. However, ten sessions of psychotherapy are only enough to break the surface for most psychological issues. If you just went through an amicable break up with your girlfriend or boyfriend, ten counseling sessions will probably do the trick. A little freaked out because you're living away from home for the first time? Ten therapy sessions are just what you need. A problem with Internet pornography? Then you need to settle in for the long haul.

Logan was a college student who came to me after exhausting his ten sessions at the Bible college. Logan was a good kid, athletic, with good grades, plenty of friends, and no history of getting in trouble. Some people might cock an eyebrow at how many hours he spent playing Call of Duty, but it didn't seem to impair his functioning in other areas, so I saw no reason to worry.

Logan's relationship with pornography started over the Thanksgiving break of his sophomore year. He had decided to stick around school over the holiday. He wanted to get a head start on his reading before finals week. Besides, he was from Peoria, Illinois, and preferred not to spend half his break fighting airport crowds and twiddling his thumbs through flight delays. He had his room and practically the whole campus to himself.

By Saturday, Logan had read several hundred pages and was sick of studying. He played Call of Duty for a few hours, but he still felt antsy. He had cabin fever. He took a walk around the empty campus, hoping to run into a familiar face. No luck. He grabbed a sandwich at Quiznos and went back to his room. Then he started surfing the Internet.

While scrolling through a message board at one of his favorite gaming sites, an advertisement popped up in the corner. It was a lingerie ad. Later, he would tell me that he clicked the ad impulsively, without thinking. He described it as a reflex, like blinking. After a few minutes of looking at ladies in their underwear, Logan felt the urge to see more. With little hesitation or reflection, he left the lingerie site and went in search of more revealing images.

It was his first time looking at pornography. He went into the trance described by so many men who become swept up in the stream of images flowing through the Internet. He kept clicking and clicking, exploring new options. Many times, he would see something repulsive and back away. However, there were plenty of "soft" images that he enjoyed. Before he knew it, he was masturbating. By the time he finished, he was mortified.

He dropped to his knees and begged God for forgiveness, vowing never to do that again. He managed to make it for six weeks. Then he made it for a month. When he could make it for no more than a week between episodes, he knew that he was in trouble. He confessed to his best friend, who agreed to hold him accountable. His use of pornography decreased, though it didn't disappear.

Logan had what I think of as a "hot motor." He was restless. He didn't have ADHD, he wasn't manic, and he didn't have an anxiety disorder, but he would get jumpy if he didn't stay busy. Logan needed to move or focus on something. It also became clear that he was very, um, heterosexual. Logan liked women. A lot. A cute girl in class was a huge distraction. However, Logan got nervous about crossing the "friend zone" with girls. Early in therapy, we discovered that one of the most effective ways to keep him away from porn was to get him to pursue a woman in an honest, open way. Before that, however, a cute girl would just make him agitated.

Logan was careful to cover his tracks when he looked at porn. He used some a special website that prevented any record of his online activity from appearing on the school's servers. He always cleared his browser history and got rid of anything pornographic websites might leave behind. He followed this practice diligently, except for one time.

Logan thought his roommate wouldn't be back from class for over an hour, so he was shocked when he heard a key in the door. He quit his web browser and pulled up his email. Problem solved.

The door opened. It wasn't his roommate. It was the RA.

"What's up, Keith?" asked Logan. Logan was pretty sure that the RA wasn't allowed into his room, but he didn't mention it. Keith didn't respond well to confrontation.

"I need to look at your computer, Logan."

What? Logan was definitely sure that wasn't okay.

"Why?"

"Somebody said they heard some things that sounded like a porn video, so I need to take a look."

"I'm not sure that's okay," said Logan. "That's kind of an invasion of my privacy."

"The Student Handbooks give the RA permission to search an Internet device if there's suspicion of improper use," Keith said. "If you don't let me look, you'll be disciplined anyway."

"Fine, go ahead." He had been using the website that would cover his tracks, so it didn't matter.

Keith sat down at Logan's iMac and pulled up the web browser. Then Logan's head went light. He had forgotten to use the special website. Everything he had been looking at was there for Keith to see. *How could I be so stupid?* thought Logan.

Keith shook his head and sighed.

"I'm really disappointed in you, Logan."

Logan stared at the ground in silence. Nothing he could say would help.

"I have to write this up and send it to the Student Disciplinary Committee. I also have to cut off Internet access to your room. You and your roommate will have to use the library if you need to get online."

That was going to go over great with his roommate.

"What happens now?"

The RA glared at him. "That's up to the Disciplinary Committee. I'd start praying hard for God's grace if I were you."

Logan believed that lying was a sin, so when the Disciplinary Committee asked him how long he had been looking at pornography over the school's Internet, he told them the truth. The Committee said that he could remain enrolled in college on two conditions. The first was that he had to get counseling for his "pornography addiction."

*****

Logan told me he was addicted to pornography in the first minute of our first session. After this confession, he only made eye contact with me when I greeted him at the beginning of the session and told him goodbye at the end. His shame was so thick that it made the room feel airless and stale.

I hate stuffy rooms.

"You're not addicted to pornography," I said about a month into therapy.

"That's not what the counselor at school told me," said Logan.

"She was wrong," I said. "She's a great lady, but she was wrong."

He lifted his gaze from the floor and looked at me for the first time in weeks.

"I hope you're right," said Logan.

I smiled at him.

"I'm wrong all the time," I said, "but I don't think I am this time. Your porn use is more of a symptom than a disease."

"So what's the disease?" he asked.

"I don't know," I said. "You might not even have one."

*****

A symptom is a natural reaction to an assault on our mental and physical systems. In this sense, a compulsion to look at pornography is almost always the symptom of a deeper problem.

Notice I used the word "compulsion" instead of "addiction." There's a reason for that. There's a big difference between a compulsion and an addiction, and it is high time Christian folks learned what it is.

A compulsion is any behavior that reduces anxiety. It's an unhealthy way of relieving or avoiding stress. Compulsions dispel tension immediately, but they are not healthy coping skills or relaxation techniques. Common compulsions include binge behaviors like overeating, alcohol abuse, excessive exercising, playing video games for ten hours, floating through online social media all night, watching nine episodes of a television show in a row, and, yes, looking at Internet pornography.

Now let's distinguish a compulsion from an addiction. While a compulsion can certainly be habit-forming and difficult to stop, it is possible for most people to control a compulsion. For example, most people with a compulsion to look at Internet pornography have some control over it.

Those of you who didn't just hurl the book across the room are saying, "You're an idiot, Steve. I know [fill in the blank], who masturbated to pornography three or four times a week. They could *not* control their behavior."

Sure they could. Though your friend certainly had a problem, they could control their problem within limits. For example, most (though not all) people who have a problem with Internet porn don't view it at work or school. They can control their urges until they get home. They can also go for extended periods of time if Internet access is not available and still function normally, though they might experience increased anxiety. For example, if someone with a compulsion to look at porn went camping for a week they would probably be fine. In fact, there is a good chance they would have less desire to look at porn when they returned from the camping trip.

An addict, on the other hand, cannot control his urges. If someone with a bona fide addiction to Internet pornography went camping for a week, they would go nuts. They would look for excuses to leave. They would find a way to sneak pornography on the trip and create opportunities to use it. For an addict, looking at pornography is not just about relieving anxiety, though anxiety and stress increase their urges. Addicts need to look at pornography regardless of their stress level. They will look at pornography at work, at school, in a public library, on a bus, and while visiting a friend. They plan their lives around using pornography. Whereas someone with a compulsion tends to use pornography during certain weak periods, an addict *always* wants to look at pornography.

Here's a simple way to understand it: With a compulsion, anxiety, stress, and sexual tension result in a desire to look at pornography. With an addiction, the constant need to consume pornography *creates* anxiety, stress, and sexual tension.

Every single client I've seen for pornography issues walked into my office with the word "addiction" on his lips. Less than one in twenty of those men had a bona fide addiction to pornography. The rest had compulsions. Please don't misunderstand me, a compulsion is a serious problem that requires serious work. However, if a client thinks he's an addict, he begins therapy at a disadvantage. He thinks that he has a debilitating disease. He thinks his sexuality is broken. He's a pervert, a *sex addict* for whom healthy, holy intimacy will forever be a challenge. We have to spend the first few weeks of therapy getting rid of that label.

What's worse, a lot of the clients I see don't even have compulsions. They just got unlucky because they are facing a problem new to human history: instantly accessible and free pornography.

Let's back into this. Your sex drive is like hunger. It's a normal biological process. It serves a function—specifically, reproduction. Since God is loving, creative, and generous, God paired the satisfaction of many key biological needs with pleasure. I'm not just talking about the relief of pain or tension, by the way. If it were a simple matter of survival and evolution, pain relief would be sufficient. For example, when you need food, you experience the discomfort of hunger pangs. When you eat, you experience relief of that discomfort. God could have made the process end there. Instead, he paired the relief of hunger with pleasure. In fact, you can get pleasure from food without even being hungry. That's what dessert is all about. You might be stuffed to the point bursting after Thanksgiving dinner, but you'll still take a slice of pumpkin pie.

The same is true of our sex drive. It serves a biological function. Not just a normal one, but a crucial one. No sex drive, no more people. We don't spore. Seeds don't fly out of a person's nose and then grow into brand new humans. Sex is a part of the life cycle, but it also feels good in its own right, like eating. Just like you relish a delicious calorie fest even though your body would get by just fine on a little bit of lean protein and a green thing, sex can feel good even when it doesn't result in reproduction.

Church history is filled with people who have said that pleasure apart from function is sin, from the first century Gnostics, to the third century Rigorists, to the seventeenth century Jansenists. They say if you eat for pleasure, it's sin (Nelson, 1978). If you have sex for pleasure, it's sin. The Church keeps branding such theology heresy, yet it still keeps popping up in different forms. Still, the powerful pleasure associated with things like eating and sex raises some problems.

Let's stick with the eating example for now. If you eat sweets, salts, and fats nonstop, you're in trouble. Most people don't eat themselves into ruin because there are three powerful safeguards against non-stop unhealthy eating. First, if you binge on cheese fries and donuts, you're going to feel like crap. You'll either feel ill, or your brain will sound an alarm saying, "Your stomach has reached its crap capacity for today!"

The second problem is scarcity of resources. We need money to buy food and space to store it. In other words, the amount of food available to you at any one time has limits.

Third, social norms control eating to some extent. My cheese fries and donut example probably sounded ridiculous to you because most people would be embarrassed to eat such a meal in public. Furthermore, being morbidly obese carries a social stigma. Though it's not unusual for someone to carry around a few extra pounds, our culture frowns on obesity. It's an overt sign that you overeat.

Until the early 1990s, pornography shared all three of these limits with binge eating. Before the Internet, someone had to seek out pornography, usually in a way that exposed them. They had to go to an adult bookstore. They had to ask for the dirty magazine behind the counter. They had to order something through the mail. They also had to store the pornography somewhere because it was a physical object like a videotape, DVD, or magazine. It was all but impossible to hide porn use completely. Also, they had to spend money if they wanted pornography. If they wanted any sort of variety, they would have to spend a lot of money. As with eating, abuse of our sex drive was limited by available resources and potential embarrassment.

Now the only limit pornography use shares with binge eating is the physical limitation. It's physically impossible to look at porn and masturbate without stopping. Otherwise, the Internet has erased old restrictions forever. The Internet burst the dam and flooded the world with porn. It's naive to think that someone, especially a male, has the willpower to resist all the time. Nevertheless, Christian leaders, including mental health professionals who should know better, accuse the flood victims of being addicts with hungry eyes and lustful hearts. Men who had no intention whatsoever of pursuing pornography found it pursuing them. Most of them run from it as hard as they can, but it's the rare man who doesn't eventually stumble or tire of the chase.

Am I excusing the use of pornography? Absolutely not. It's unhealthy. It's bad for relationships. It promotes the objectification of other people. It's a sin, just like gluttony. However, I believe that a problem with pornography is not as personal or individual as the Church makes it out to be. Most people who struggle with Internet pornography are not especially lustful. In fact, most of them *would have never struggled with porn at all if the Internet did not exist.* Contrast this with an alcoholic. If an alcoholic does not have any booze, they will go find more. Get rid of the Internet for someone that struggles with porn, and their use of pornography will usually disappear.

Internet pornography is a social problem, and the Church needs a social response. Where is it? Where is the lobby in Washington for legislation that makes it more difficult for someone to access Internet pornography? It's impossible to shut it down completely, but there are dozens of ways to make it harder to access porn. Christian-backed lobbies have spent millions of dollars to fight things like abortion and bans on school prayer, yet little has been done to oppose one of the largest spiritual and mental health crises of our time. The most common strategy is to blame the victims of this crisis by telling them they have lustful hearts and calling them addicts. We tell people drowning in a flood that they are just bad swimmers.

Again, don't misunderstand me; anyone who has a problem with Internet pornography must take personal responsibility. If there's a flood, you'd better know how to swim. Those who struggle with pornography must repent and ask for God's grace and guidance. They must explore the causes of the behavior and develop ways to control it. They need to seek help. But they need their Church to stop making *them* the enemy and support them in fighting the real enemy.

Young men struggling with Internet porn come to me for therapy on a regular basis. My clients are surprised when I don't react to their problem with shock and horror. I'm far more likely to give them a hard time for short-changing the power of God's grace on the occasions when they "stumble." I try to help them find something that's more exciting and meaningful than Internet pornography. Rather than merely emptying them of their struggle with pornography, I encourage them to fill up their lives with the adventure God has in store for them. In my experience, it's more effective and more fun than fighting the battle with shame.

Logan and I worked hard to overcome his problem with Internet pornography. Though our work went well, he didn't really need my help. Help came through grace he never believed possible, from a source he never could have imagined.

*****

The second condition of Logan's probation was that he had to live off campus.

After an expensive lawsuit, the school began what they called "The Grace and Tolerance Initiative." The school no longer expelled students who violated the school's "Code of Christian Conduct" unless the violation was something egregious, such as a felony. Instead, they banned students from living in campus housing. Since the college required students to live in campus housing all four years, this was more of a scarlet letter than it might have been at another college.

Logan was from Arizona, so living at home and commuting wasn't an option. On the brink of homelessness, Logan ended up staring at a bulletin board that advertised off-campus living opportunities. Only five pieces of paper adorned the ragged board. Three advertised opportunities for "FEMALES ONLY." The fourth one was out of his price range.

The last flyer was more attractive than the rest. The graphics looked almost professional. Instead of slats of paper on the bottom with contact information for potential tenants to rip away, a tiny pocket filled with business cards hung on the laminated sign. The ad looked great. Logan knew who put it there without even reading it.

The ad was from Benedict. Benedict needed two roommates, male or female. There was no way Logan was moving in with Benedict. He'd move out to Pomona and live on an alpaca farm before setting foot in Benedict's house.

"What are you in for?" said a voice from behind.

Logan turned to see a stocky Asian guy. Logan was pretty sure he was Korean. He looked a little bit old for a college student, maybe twenty-six or twenty-seven.

"Let me guess," said the man. "It's either porn or booze. But you don't look like the drinking type, so I'm guessing porn."

Logan's jaw dropped.

"How did you–"

The man waved a hand and laughed.

"It's not like I'm a Jedi Knight or something. Only those of us who have been banished from the flock end up looking at this board. The only things anyone ever gets punished for in the Code of Conduct have to do with sex, drugs, or booze, so it was an easy guess. I mean, you never see anyone lined up here for gossip or refusing the poor or failing to love their neighbor as they would themselves. You and I are in the vice squad."

Logan couldn't help but smile.

"Okay, well then how about you?" asked Logan.

The man shook his head.

"I wish it had been porn or booze. I got divorced, and I couldn't convince the Student Disciplinary Committee that I tried hard enough to prevent it. Of course, when your wife splits during the honeymoon and no one in her family will tell you where she is or let you talk to her, it's kind of hard to reconcile."

"Ouch," said Logan. "You're right. Booze or porn would have been better."

"And cheaper," said the man. "And I'd only feel ashamed over porn, not ashamed *and* stupid because the love of my life devoured my heart and bailed on me without warning. And my whole family wouldn't be treating me like a leper. So, yeah, porn or booze would have been better."

The man offered his hand to Logan.

"I'm Eliot."

"I'm Logan."

"So," said Eliot, "looks like we're stuck with Benedict."

That took Logan aback.

"I don't know, man," said Logan.

"What bothers you?" asked Eliot. "Is it that he's gay or that I'm Asian?"

"What? No. I'm not . . . Hey, where do you get off calling a black guy you just met racist. That's pretty bold."

"Just homophobic, then?" said Eliot.

That made Logan angry.

"Just because I believe what the Bible says doesn't mean that I am homophobic."

"Okay, then, do you think using pornography is wrong?"

"Of course. I've repented, and I'm in counseling."

"I think using porn is wrong, and I'm willing to live with you. And I promise I'm not racist."

"Let me guess," said Logan, "one of your best friends is black."

"No," he said, "but one of my ex-girlfriends is. My life would be a whole lot better right now if I'd had the sense to stick with her instead of marrying the woman who just ate my soul."

Logan started to think Eliot might be a scarier roommate than a gay man.

"Listen," said Eliot. "I'm not crazy about living with Benedict, either. Having a gay friend might be okay, but living with a gay guy could be very weird. What if he sees me naked? What if he brings his boyfriend around? That would gross me out. But, if you and I move in together, at least the straight guys will outnumber him. We'll watch each other's back. Besides, it's a whole lot cheaper than anything else out there."

Logan thought for a moment, frowning.

"I mean, I guess that makes sense. I'll think about it."

"Have you seen the house?" asked Eliot.

"No."

"I have. After one look, you'll move in."

Logan and Eliot arranged to visit Benedict's house together. The house was beyond anything a college student could hope for. It was a small craftsman style house in Sierra Madre with three bedrooms. The outside was red and grey. Inside, Benedict had painted each room a different color. Benedict described the theme as "kind of a mishmash of art deco and steampunk, but I tried not to go overboard." Logan had no idea what that meant, but the place looked cool.

But Logan had decided to move in the instant he walked through the front door. After Benedict let them in, Logan's eyes landed on the most sophisticated entertainment and gaming system he had ever seen. Mounted in the center of a wall was a fifty-inch back-lit LCD screen. Beneath it were two Bose speakers that projected surround sound, which saved you the trouble of littering the room with speakers. All the latest video and audio technology sat neatly aligned on a shelf beneath the screen. But what almost made Logan swoon was the fact that all the latest consoles from Microsoft, Sony, and Nintendo stood in a neat row beneath the massive monitor. Beside them stood a shelf packed with games.

Logan asked Benedict, "Does this come with the rent? If it doesn't, I'll pay extra."

Benedict laughed. Logan expected some kind of feminine giggle, but it was just a regular guy's laugh.

"It comes with the rent," said Benedict. "You guys are welcome to use it whenever I 'm not playing. And you're always welcome to join in when I am."

"What's your favorite game?" asked Eliot.

"Call of Duty," said Benedict.

"I will totally smoke you at Call of Duty," said Eliot.

"Big talk, big man," said Benedict. "We'll have to see about that. What about you, Logan?"

Logan just smiled and said, "I play a little."

Logan knew he would destroy both of them. He was so good that people would leave games when they saw his screen name appear on the roster of the opposing team. He had won tournaments on campus and even considered professional gaming for a little while.

"Then how about this," said Benedict. "If you guys like the house and the rent is right, come over on Friday night. We'll have some pizza and play Call of Duty for a while. Then, if everyone decides it's a good fit, we'll shake hands."

Nobody had to think twice.

On Friday, Eliot picked up Logan and drove him to Benedict's house. When Benedict greeted them at the door, an aroma hit Logan that made his stomach growl.

"What are you cooking?" asked Eliot.

"Pizza, like I said," Benedict replied.

Logan had assumed that Benedict meant they would be ordering pizza. Instead, he and Eliot followed Benedict into the kitchen to find three large homemade pizzas cooling on the stove. One was drowning in different types of cheese. Another was covered with fresh-looking tomatoes, mushrooms, and black olives. The last was like something out of Logan's vision of heaven: a smoking round mound of cheese, pepperoni, sausage, and bacon. A pig had given its life for this pizza.

"Holy cow," said Eliot. "Benedict, what did you do?"

"I didn't know what you guys liked," said Benedict. "So I made a little of everything. It's no big deal. What we don't eat will feed me for a couple of days. Drinks are in the fridge."

Logan and Eliot grabbed beer out of the fridge. Benedict said a quick blessing, and they attacked the pizza. It was the best pizza Logan had ever tasted outside of Chicago.

"So," said Benedict. "Let's get some things out of the way before we start playing Call of Duty."

Logan almost choked on his last bite. He wasn't ready to talk about the gay thing yet.

"You guys are probably wondering why the rent is so low and how I can afford all of this stuff," said Benedict.

Whew.

"There are three different answers. First, I have a full-time job as a floor manager at Target. The pay isn't bad, and I get a really good discount on everything. I'm almost done with classes, and I take everything online, so it works out."

"Did you get that television at Target?" asked Eliot with his mouth full.

"Yeah, but I had to get it online."

"Awesome," Eliot said, taking a bite of pizza.

"Second, I've had a hard time finding roommates, so I'm willing to pay a little more. I also have the biggest room, which takes up most of the upstairs."

"Works for me," said Eliot. He then belched and went to the refrigerator for another beer.

"Finally, my father is an attorney in Michigan, a pretty successful one. Two years ago, he set up a trust fund, and I get payments from that every month."

"That must be nice," said Eliot. "Why did your dad set up a trust fund for you two years ago."

"So he would never have to see me again."

Eliot's face wrinkled into a frown.

"What? Why?"

"Because that's when I came out."

"Dude," said Eliot. "That sucks. I'm sorry."

Benedict gave a soft smile. "Thanks. I'm starting to get used to it. Kind of."

Logan didn't say anything. He noticed that he was peeling the label off his bottle of Sam Adams.

"Logan, do you have any questions about anything."

Logan shrugged and looked down. "Not really."

"Do you know why I don't live on campus?"

"I guess they kicked you off, like they did me and Eliot."

"Nope."

Logan's head popped up.

"Really? But I thought-"

"That they kicked me off because I was gay? They don't really do that. They would have had to catch me . . . doing something. No, I got special permission to live off campus."

"Why?" asked Eliot.

"I came out to a girl who I thought was my best friend. I asked her not to tell anyone. She said she wouldn't, but she did. When it got back to my roommate, he refused to live with me anymore. Nobody else wanted to live with me, either. I could have gotten a single room, but I still would have had to deal with the bathrooms emptying out every time I went to take a shower. It was just easier this way, and I think the college administrators understood that."

Logan frowned. He had heard a lot of rumors about Benedict getting kicked off campus, all of which involved sensationalist tales of homosexual sex. How could people be so cruel?

"I . . . I'm sorry about that," said Logan.

"Thanks, man."

"Any other touchy subjects before we cut loose on some pixelated carnage?" asked Eliot.

"I'm afraid so," said Benedict. "I'm not really big on rules, but just a couple of guidelines."

"Fire away," said Eliot.

"First, I know why both of you got kicked out."

"What? How?" said Logan.

"Eliot told me."

Eliot gave a toothy smile and then slapped his hand over his mouth. "Oops!" he said.

"Hey! I did not give you permission to say anything!"

"Give me a break," said Eliot. "Like he wasn't going to find out anyway. And he had the right to know. You could have been kicked off campus for stealing or murdering puppies or something."

"He has a point," said Benedict.

Logan got up in a huff and went to the fridge for another beer. He popped it open and sat down.

"Fine!" he said. "So what's your point?"

"My point is that I don't think living off campus is an excuse for any of us to forget that we're Christians who live according to a higher calling. So, if you're going to live here Logan, I want you to use the Internet only on your laptop out in the main living area."

Logan didn't like that. Coming from anyone else, he might have refused. But Benedict had a matter-of-fact way of saying it that made the issue lighter, less serious. He wasn't making a big deal out of it, just making a suggestion.

"That's fine," said Logan. "Or I'll leave the door open to my room."

"Just as good," said Benedict.

Eliot was laughing.

"No more private love sessions for you!"

"As for you, sir," said Benedict, giving Eliot a sharp look.

"What? What did I do? I can't help it if my wife left me."

"Really? How long did you guys date before you got engaged?"

Eliot flushed.

"Why?"

"*How long?*"

"Um, three months."

Logan's face collapsed into his arms. Soon his whole torso was shaking with muted laughter.

Eliot's flippant demeanor vanished.

"Hey, that's not funny!"

"You're right," said Benedict. "It's not. So, while you're living here, I think it would be a good idea for you to spend more time with friends and groups of people and not date for a little while. When you do start dating, maybe you should expect it to last for at least six months before even thinking about engagement."

Eliot looked back and forth between Logan and Benedict with his mouth open.

"What kind of cuckoo's nest have I landed in?" shouted Eliot.

He sighed and threw up his hands.

"Fine, but I'm moving out if this gets any weirder."

Logan looked at Benedict.

"What about you?"

"What about me?" asked Benedict.

"Can we make suggestions for you?"

"Like what?"

"Like you can't make out with guys or something?"

"That's . . . more complicated. But you don't have to worry about that for now."

All this frank talk had made Logan bold.

"Why shouldn't we have to worry about it?"

Benedict paused.

"Okay, why not. I might as well get this out of the way, too. I haven't figured everything out about my sexuality yet, but I know this much: I am not attracted to women at all, and I'm definitely attracted to men. I also know that I want to follow Christ. I'm still trying to figure out what that means for me. The other thing that I know for sure is that it is extremely difficult to lead a holy life and be active in the gay community in Los Angeles. It's wild, it's promiscuous, and it's not what I need. Even a lot of gay folks that claim to be Christians don't lead what I would consider a Christian lifestyle. That's why I wanted roommates from school. You guys seem cool, so I hope this works out."

Silence. Logan nursed his beer, trying to get his head around all that had happened in the course of one meal.

"Benedict," said Eliot. "I have never met anyone like you in my entire life. This is going to be an adventure."

"Well, not too much of an adventure, which leads me to my last point."

"Which is?" said Logan.

"I don't find either of you remotely attractive, so you can both relax."

They laughed until Logan thought that Eliot might hyperventilate. Then they washed up the dishes from dinner and went into the living room to play Call of Duty.

They played until two a.m. Benedict annihilated everyone.

*****

It didn't take long for word to spread about Logan's new living situation. The rumors started soon after. The story that Logan was addicted to porn became a tale of addiction to *gay* porn. The worst tongue-waggers said that Logan moved in with two other gay guys, and they were having gay orgies. Acquaintances and even a few longtime friends avoided eye contact and stopped talking to him. Logan's dating prospects went from meager to nonexistent.

A cadre of defiant friends still remained. His former roommate, furious that he lost Logan in exchange for a new roommate that was a "lifeless OCD freak that keeps the thermostat at the temperature of death," remained steadfastly on his side. Some guys who'd been gaming with him since freshman year also stuck with him. As a show of solidarity, they asked if they could come by his house and hang out sometime. When Logan asked Benedict about it, Benedict was thrilled.

Eliot and Logan had become accustomed to Benedict cooking for them. They would come home from work or school to find a meal waiting for them. They never took it for granted. They always did the dishes and got shopping lists from Benedict whenever they went to the store. But they left the cooking and entertaining to Benedict because he was gifted. When Eliot's parents had come over for dinner, they embarrassed Eliot by remarking over and over that Benedict was better at cooking, cleaning, fixing things than Eliot had ever been. Eliot's mother kissed Benedict and called him "such a delightful, handsome young man."

When Benedict found out that Logan invited half a dozen people over to play video games, he pulled out all the stops. He started preparing days in advance.

"Dude," said Logan, "it's just a few guys."

"I don't care," said Benedict. "This is going to be awesome."

By the time the evening arrived, the house and backyard were immaculate. Food and beverage stations were everywhere. When Logan's friends arrived, they were gob smacked.

"This is the coolest house I have ever seen," they said.

"Logan, you do not deserve this place."

"Wow. How do I get kicked off campus?"

They ate, drank, laughed, played video games, and then laughed some more. By one a.m., everyone was out on the back porch, deep in conversation. They talked about movies, music, love, and God. Everyone was still there at three a.m.

"You know," said Benedict, yawning, "we should do this again."

"We should do this every week," said one of the guys.

"Don't kid around," said Eliot, "because I could."

"Well," said Benedict. "Why don't we?"

Logan interceded. "Guys, we will totally do this again, but I don't know if Benedict would be up for this much excitement all the time. You might notice that he goes over the top when it comes to entertaining guests."

"Benedict rules," said one of Logan's gaming friends.

"How about we make it like a regular Bible study and gaming night?" said Benedict. "You guys should invite girls next time."

"Girls!" said Eliot.

"I didn't mean you," said Benedict and Eliot socked him in the arm.

"I don't know if girls would be down with the gaming," said Logan.

"Well, then," said Benedict. "We'll have to do this twice a week, I guess. One night could be Bible study, gaming, and pizza. Then another night we'll have like a pot-luck and hangout thing in the backyard."

"Thursday night Bible-gaming and Saturday night hangout," said Eliot.

"Done," said Benedict.

Just like that, Logan, Eliot, and Benedict's house became the focal point of off-campus social life. Everyone at school started referring to it simply as "The House." After six-weeks, they had to institute an online sign-up list because the crowds got too large. What started as a small-group Bible study on Thursday nights became a mini-church service with over thirty people. Eliot would play guitar, and they would sing some songs. Then someone would give a ten-minute talk. A few different people spoke, but everyone came to hear Benedict. He had a way with words and keen insights into Scripture. To Logan and Eliot's surprise, he knew a little bit of Greek and Hebrew and unpacked new meanings from well-worn passages. After the talk, people would break up into groups and talk about whatever they wanted. Things would wrap up with time in prayer. Then it was off to the video games. People had to bring in their own monitors and consoles to accommodate the crowds. To the chagrin of the ladies, the gaming was non-negotiable on Bible study night. To the chagrin of the gentlemen, games such as Dance Revolution began usurping Call of Duty.

Saturday nights were all about food and fun. That's where Logan met Candace, who fell harder and faster for him than any woman he'd ever met. She had dark hair, Caribbean blue eyes, and an irrepressible personality. He was definitely attracted to her, but he had never met a girl who flirted so aggressively. She was touchy-feely to the point where Logan didn't know if he liked her or if she just turned him on so much that he couldn't think straight.

One Saturday night, Logan talked to Candace until everyone else had gone home. She noticed that her ride had left and asked Logan to drive her home. He agreed without hesitation. When she told him that her roommate was out of town, he had little illusion about what waited in store once they arrived at her dorm room.

"Wait for me on the front porch," he told her. "Let me go get my keys." Logan dashed to his room, found his keys, and galloped toward the front door.

"Logan."

It was Benedict. He was sitting on the couch watching *Kitchen Nightmares*, one of his favorite shows.

"What's up?" said Logan.

"If you take sexual advantage of that girl in any way, shape, or form, I'm going to rip your arms off and beat you over the head with them until you are unconscious. I will then load you into my car, drive ninety miles per hour down the 210 freeway, and push you out of the car without stopping."

Benedict stuck a Dorito in his mouth and crunched it down. Then he turned back to his television show. Logan stammered for a response, but nothing came.

"Candace is waiting for me," he finally said, and bolted out the door.

Logan drove Candace home and walked her up to her dorm room. When she tried to pull him inside, he had to pull back hard to keep from tumbling in. How could such a tiny girl be so strong?

"Need some help?" said a female voice from behind. A girl stood in the doorway of the room across the hall, shaking her head.

"Could you?" asked Logan.

"Sure," she said.

The girl walked into Candace's room and took her by the shoulders. Candace gave her a dirty look. "Candace, sweetie, we've talked about this."

Logan didn't want to hear the rest.

"Goodnight, Candace!" he said, then scurried away.

As Logan drove back home, he noticed an odd feeling or, rather, the absence of one. Candace might have been a little wild for him, but she was hot. Still, Logan would have refused her advances, even without Benedict's playful threats of violence. He wasn't even sure how he felt about her, so hooking up was out of the question. But that didn't change the fact that she turned him on. Normally, Logan would have been fitful with unfulfilled desire, tense and eager for some kind of release. The urge to search the Internet for arousing images had always come in moments like these. Where was that urge now?

Tears started to form as a realization rushed in. *No, it's not possible*, he thought. *That can't be right.* Logan looked at the calendar on his phone and started counting. He hadn't looked at pornography in over three months.

He pulled into the driveway and ran in the front door. Benedict was still sitting on the couch.

"Benny, man, you aren't going to believe this."

"*'Benny?'* Since when do you call me Benny?"

"I don't know. Since now."

"Since never. Don't do it again."

"Sorry. I'm just excited."

"What's up? Did you kiss that Candace girl? You better have behaved yourself."

"No, no. That's not it. I haven't looked at porn since I've lived here. Not even once. In fact, I haven't even thought about it."

Benedict smiled and put his hand up for a high five.

"Excellent work, sir!"

"It's crazy, because it's not like I've even been trying . . . I've just been. . . I don't know."

"Living with people and loving it?"

Logan thought for a minute.

"Yeah. How did you know?"

Benedict's eyes started to glisten, and he swallowed.

"Because the same thing has been happening to me."

"I don't understand. You don't really seem like you need to be held accountable for anything."

"Oh, I do, believe me," said Benedict. "But don't go assuming it's about the gay thing. I can be selfish and mean. I've had a real problem with being bitter. You guys do more than you know to help me stay on top of that, but that's not really what I mean. I just feel . . . "

Benedict started to cry. Logan sat down and put his arm around him. On the television, Chef Gordon Ramsay was yelling at a cowering short-order cook.

"Isn't it a little late for all this drama?" said a hoarse voice.

Eliot stumbled out of his bedroom with a blanket wrapped around his head and shoulders. He collapsed on the couch on the other side of Benedict. He leaned into him and closed his eyes.

"You guys woke me up, and I started eavesdropping," he said. "I figured that was probably a sin, so I should just join in."

Benedict laughed through his tears.

"Go on," said Logan.

"I've been without family for two years. I've been without a church for just as long. The ones I like won't accept me, and the rest are all too liberal for me. The only safe, solid place in my life has been my job at Target and, believe me, that gets old after a while. You guys brought people to my house. You made it a home. You brought church here, exactly the kind I needed. You guys have given me — it's embarrassing to say. . ."

"We are your brothers," said Logan. "We are your family. We should have been that before we moved in. I'm sorry it took a cool gaming system for me to realize that."

"Yeah," said Eliot, yawning. "And I'm sorry my crazy wife had to leave me before I realized that."

Benedict punched him in the arm.

"So, you guys are my family?" asked Benedict. He asked like he was afraid of the answer.

"You bet," said Logan.

"Of course," said Eliot. "A lot better than the family my wife and I made. You've stuck with me longer. You're a better cook, too."

They sat on the couch in silence, listening to Gordon Ramsay explain how a restaurant could spice up their Chilean sea bass.

"Benedict," said Logan. "What do you want to do after you graduate?"

"I'm not sure," said Benedict. "But I know what I wanted to be . . . before."

"You wanted to be a pastor, didn't you?" said Logan.

Benedict nodded with tears flowing down his cheeks.

"Yeah," he said. "I don't know if that will ever happen now."

"It already has," said Logan. "You're our pastor."

"Does that make us sheep in his flock?" asked Eliot.

"Absolutely," said Logan.

"Baaaaaa!" said Eliot.

Benedict and Logan pounced on Eliot and wrestled him to the floor. They took turns punching him in the arm until he shouted, "I submit! Tap out, tap out!" Then Benedict made a pizza covered in meat, even though it was almost four a.m. They ate, talked, and played Call of Duty until the sun came up.

*****

We have to accept something difficult: Healthy, holy sexuality looks different for everyone.

That sentence probably bothered you. Just writing it was difficult. I'm tempted to clarify, qualify, and assure you that there are lines we shouldn't cross. And, yes, I do believe in absolutes. I believe in sin, but that's not the point. Working together to create healthy, holy sexuality means understanding that one person's journey will be different from yours. I cannot tell you God's will for every person's sexuality. I can only tell you this: No one can figure it out alone. We need God, and we need each other.

You might notice that I didn't have many psychological insights to add about Logan's journey. That's because I didn't add very much to his journey. I helped here and there, but Logan didn't really need a shrink. He needed a community. He needed his life to be about more than just him. In Eliot and Benedict, he found two people who felt just as alone and fragile. Their relationship wasn't about accountability. They didn't spend all their time talking about their struggles. They built a brotherhood around friendship.

Logan's disease was not pornography addiction: It was isolation. Benedict and Eliot helped cure his disease, and the symptoms went away. While discipline and self-control will always be fundamental to holy, healthy sexuality, they have nothing to do with why God created us. He created us to be in relationship with Him and each other. If we can master that, the rest will work itself out.

Chapter Seven:
"Let's Make a Scene"

"Being a Christian is less about cautiously avoiding sin than about courageously and actively doing God's will."

–Dietrich Bonhoeffer

During my first year of graduate school, I got a crush on girl we'll call Kelly. Kelly made small but inconclusive signs of reciprocating my interest. We hadn't been on a date, but we spent a lot of time together. She flirted with me and invited me to her apartment whenever she had people over. We were "hanging out," a practice fraught with peril for the smitten.

Kelly and her roommate threw a small party at the end of finals after winter quarter. Kelly invited me and a few other friends. People were imbibing distilled spirits more than usual that evening. At some point, someone decided it would be a good idea for the guests to assemble on Kelly's bed. Everyone joined in but me. I wasn't too prudish or uptight to hop on the bed with everyone; I just thought it was a stupid idea and I didn't feel like it.

I had an intermittent cigarette vice at the time, so I stepped onto the balcony of Kelly's bedroom and lit up a smoke. When I turned around and looked back at Kelly's bed, what I saw activated the fight or flight centers in my brain.

Kelly was lying next to a guy named Darren. Darren had the interpersonal boundaries of an intoxicated orangutan. He would run his hands up and down the person of any woman within reach, be she single, married, or extraterrestrial. In a moment of horror, Kelly put her head in Darren's lap. The back of her head was right next to his . . . well, you know where it was. Darren's fingers crept across Kelly's hair and neck and then progressed toward the borders of her sovereign territory. And Kelly was rubbing his legs and feet! What was the matter with her? Had someone put Drano in her mojito? Couldn't she see me out on the balcony, watching the whole thing? Did she think I was made of stone?

I started puffing on my cigarette like I was auditioning to be a coal factory. Kelly's roommate came out and asked to bum a smoke.

"What's wrong with you?" she asked.

"Look at Kelly and Darren!" I shouted.

"So?" said the girl. "They're just goofing around." She took a cigarette and left, not even bothering to smoke with me in my distress.

Just before I chained-smoked myself into terminal emphysema, my friend Ryan appeared on the balcony. He had just arrived from working late at the bookstore. His smile disappeared when he saw me inhaling toxins in record amounts.

"Dude, what's the matter?" he asked.

"It's Kelly and Darren," I said. "Look."

Ryan looked. Then he grimaced. "What is her problem?" he said. "She knows you can see her. She knows you like her. Does she want you and Darren to duel with swords for her affection or something?"

His words shook me. I had been rattling with anxiety, worried only that Kelly liked Darren more than me. Being disappointed with her never occurred to me.

"You deserve better than this nonsense," said Ryan.

That had never occurred to me, either. Why was I having a panic attack and smoking myself into an early grave over a girl who would pull something like this? Ryan was right. I deserved better, but I wouldn't have realized it without his help.

A mischievous grin spread across Ryan's face. He wasn't finished. He didn't just want me to know that I deserved better. He wanted everyone to know. "Dude," he said. "Let's make a scene."

Before I could even ask what "making a scene" entailed, Ryan flung open the balcony doors and stomped inside. "We are leaving!" he announced to the throng of revelers wallowing on Kelly's bed. Ryan marched out the front door. I followed, doing my best to look proud and indignant.

Before we made it to the street, a voice came calling from behind. Stop! Please don't go!" It was Kelly, followed by a girl rumored to have a crush on Ryan. We gently assured the girls that we would explain everything later. Then we got into Ryan's Volkswagen Rabbit and he turned on Pearl Jam. Ryan gave me a high-five, and we sped away in search of new adventures and better stories.

*****

Sexuality isn't about you. It's not about me. It's about *us*: God, you, me, and the Body of Christ, head to toe.

Other people always helped me grow in ways I never could have on my own. I would not have known what to do that night without Ryan. More important, I wouldn't have realized what I needed. It took his help for me to remember that God expects more for me, so I should expect more for myself. I never grew because of shame or fear. I only grew when I realized that God made me for something better.

What if we value healthy, holy sexuality just because that's the way God wanted it and because everything else is a cheap substitute, a fallen shadow of what God intended? By valuing sexual health and holiness, we show the world, and each other, that sexuality is something beautiful. People are beautiful. Love is beautiful. Let's make a scene of loving and prizing sexuality from the cradle to the grave. That means caring for it every step of the way. We can only do that together; no one can do it alone.

Christians must embrace themselves as sexual people *together*. This goes beyond a myopic focus on things like finding the right spouse, saving sex for marriage, homosexuality, and anything else based on fear. Let's make a show of yearning for the kind of beauty and fulfillment God wants.

How do we do that? It's simple. Notice I said "simple," not "easy." We have to unload all the shame that blocks people from feeling like sexual people made in the image of God, whether they're single or married, gay or straight. I'm not saying that no one should ever feel *guilty*. Guilt and shame are very different. Guilt says, "I'm a good person who did a bad thing." Guilt should follow sin. It helps us to repent, recover, and reconcile with those we've hurt.

Shame is more insidious. Shame says, "I did a bad thing because *I am bad*." Shame is the Devil's best friend. It creates feelings and behaviors that drive us deeper into sin. We despair of true repentance and change. We give up on the reconciliation and renewal that heals hearts, minds, and relationships. Shame makes us feel broken beyond repair. It has no place in the Body of Christ. The Church should be marked by love instead of shame, but that's harder. Shame reduces sexuality to a list of rules, while love seeks the best for everyone. Love is more work.

Do I believe sex should be saved for marriage? Yes, though I think the consequences of premarital sex, like those of all sin, are smoldering embers extinguished by the ocean of God's grace. Should kissing be saved for marriage? I don't think so . . . but *it depends*. A tiny minority of folks can't kiss someone without wanting to rip off their clothes. For these folks, a simple prohibition to save kissing for marriage still isn't enough. If their hormones redline so fast, marriage is going to be just as hard as being single. Someone like this needs support. They need to feel comfortable talking about their turbo-charged sex drive with people who won't shame them. That's the only way they can take steps toward sexual wholeness. Merely banning kissing until marriage won't help very much.

What about all the cuddling, touching, caressing, romping, and rolling around that doesn't meet the technical definition of sex? *It depends*. The Bible doesn't specify. The research is inconclusive. I can't tell you what the answer is. I can only tell you this: No one can figure it out alone. We need God, and we need each other.

We have to make a scene. We need someone to come alongside us and say, "What's the matter?" Then we need to tell them, and we need to figure it out together. Then we make a scene, showing the world and the Church that we want more from sexuality than cheap substitutes or legalistic shame. We must walk a narrow path together, even if it means walking a few extra miles in strange territory for the sake of our brothers and sisters.

The process is messy, I admit, but we shouldn't be scared. Sex shouldn't scare us. Neither should sin, though we flee from it. We flee into the arms of a Savior who has defeated sin. We will try not to sin and repent when we do. We will do our best not to fail, but we want more than that. We long for an experience of sexuality that feels like a blessing instead of a sickness for which abstinence is the treatment and marriage is the cure. We can do better, but only together.

Single sexuality is an oxymoron. Sexuality is a gift from God that we receive as a body. You're a member of that body, whether you're married or not.

Afterword

When I finished the first draft of this book, I noticed a gaping hole. Nowhere had I addressed the difficult issues divorced people face when it comes to sexuality and faith. Though divorce is part of Mia's story, it wasn't central to her journey. I needed another story dealing with the complicated and painful repercussions of divorce.

I had no idea that story would be mine.

In late 2014, my wife and I separated. Several months later, we legally divorced, and my life changed in ways I never could have imagined.

Out of respect for my ex-wife and my children, I won't get into the specifics except to say this: I didn't want it, and I fought it. There was no adultery, no domestic violence, or any other type of tabloid fodder. Some people were quick to point out that being parents of quadruplets would be hard on any marriage, but that wasn't it, either. Though raising four kids of the same age can be stressful, our children brought more joy than anything else. Neither children nor scandal destroyed our relationship. Our marriage collapsed under the weight of the same garden-variety crap that most couples endure. That's one of the reasons it was so confusing and painful. In my therapy practice, I have helped numerous couples going through far worse problems than those that ended our marriage. But I couldn't save mine.

In an instant, my whole life changed. Problems I knew about only in theory became crushing realities. I spent long, agonizing days away from my children. My social network was upended. I had to find a new place to live. My health went into decline. I had to explain what happened to family, friends, and co-workers. I became ensnared by financial problems that will take years to untangle.

And then there was sex. But we'll get to that in a minute.

Before tackling the issue of sexuality after divorce, we need to talk about everything else that happens to divorced Christians. Not only is the modern Christian Church ill-equipped to handle divorce, the Church makes things worse. For years, I had been griping about how the Church lets down divorced Christians. I didn't know how bad things really were until I started living it. Divorced persons are the lepers of modern Evangelical Christianity.

Take a look at your church bulletin on any given Sunday. Flip to the back and look over the various events, classes, and ministries being offered. For starters, you probably won't see anything offered for divorced people. But that's not the problem. The problem is that *everything else* your church offers seems expertly designed to remind divorced people that they are, in fact, divorced. Couples classes. Family events. Sunday school classes for newlyweds. Sunday school classes for couples with young children. Sunday school classes for "empty-nesters." Singles ministries emphasizing that the cut-off age is 40. Marriage enrichment retreats. "Family" picnics. The list is endless. My wife and I spent several years in a close-knit Sunday School class for parents of young kids. The day that we separated, I let her have the Sunday School class. It would have been miserably awkward attending together — for us and everyone else. In essence, I lost my closest faith community.

A study conducted by LifeWay Research revealed that only 35% of divorced churchgoers said they felt welcome at their church after their divorce. Only twenty-six percent said that Church members stayed in touch with them after the divorce. Fifty-seven percent of churchgoers began attending a different church following their divorce. Twenty-one percent of the people surveyed reported that they no longer attend church at all following the divorce (Green, 2015).

If the Church wishes to be a true Body of Christ, it needs to value and love its divorced members. A former pastor of mine came up with his own satirical beatitude that said, "Blessed are they that break a leg, for they shall receive a casserole." His point was that the church reacts well to straightforward problems like a physical injury or illness, while other, often more devastating, problems like divorce go ignored.

Yes, divorce is messy. Yes, it strains and complicates relationships within a faith community. It is hard to know what to say and how to help. But if the Church isn't up for handling the most challenging and messy problems of its people, then the Church isn't doing its job. While there were certainly people from my church who reached out to me during my divorce, it mostly felt like everyone sat back and watched it happen. Following the divorce, I felt completely lost inside my own congregation. One or two friends did what they could to make me feel welcome, but I mostly felt alone at church.

Getting divorced had a devastating impact on my identity in a multitude of ways. First, I am a Christian who believes in the permanence and sanctity of marriage except in extreme circumstances like adultery and abuse. To be clear, I am not saying that divorce is avoidable except for these circumstances; rather, I am saying that every effort possible should be made to preserve and protect marriage. Divorce should be the absolute last resort. Getting divorced changed how I thought of myself. I felt as if my status as a Christian had been downgraded. How could I feel like a good Christian and a divorced man at the same time?

Second, my professional identity was all but obliterated. I'm a psychologist who helps people with relationship problems almost every day. I am a professor in a Christian graduate school of psychology. I have authored books about dating and marriage for a Christian audience. Getting divorced diminished, perhaps even destroyed, my credibility as any kind of relationship "expert" with a Christian audience.

Finally, and most devastating, my identity as a father took a massive blow. I am still involved in my kids' lives as much as possible, but I am only with them about 20% of the time. I talk to them on the phone every day that I'm not with them, but it's not the same as seeing them, singing them to sleep, and going through the ups and downs of daily life. I cherish the time that I spend with them and make the most of it. I know they value it, too, and they love me as much, if not more, than ever. But it's hard to feel like a good father when I'm separated from my kids 80% of the time. I miss my kids constantly when I'm not with them. More than anything, I worry about how all this is impacting them.

Did you notice that I haven't mentioned sex at all? In the face of all these other losses, sex seems of little consequence right now. I still experience sexual desire, but it is little more than an annoyance compared to everything else I've lost. Even if it did matter to me, I would have no clue what to do about it. I have no idea who I am as a sexual person anymore.

I still have sexual desires. If I never get married again, does that mean I adopt a spiritual discipline of chastity? I don't know, but that's not my main concern. My biggest problem is that *part of me has fallen for the same crap I have been warning you about throughout this entire book.* An emotional, irrational part of me thinks, "I have already had sex. I am no longer a virgin. What does it matter if I have sex again with someone else, whether we are married or not?" Part of me is still stuck back in middle school, only able to conceive of sex as a one-time, either-or proposition. This part of me sabotages my theological sensibilities and spiritual reflections. It tells me that it doesn't matter if I have sex or don't; since I have already had sex and I'm now divorced, everything is pointless.

Yet, it's not pointless, and I know that. I know this because God has sent people in my life to remind me. My friends and family have been my salvation during this long, dark period. People like Ryan, Kevin, Lauren, Jeff, and Mari keep reminding me, sometimes just through their friendship, that there is still hope. My parents and sisters have been more steadfast in their love and care than ever. I'd be in big trouble without them. I would have given up hope.

Hope is, at long last, seeping back into my life. My friends and family surrounded the tight, dark cell that became my life and loved me in my worst moments. Their love trickled in through the cracks and started dripping from the walls. It has not banished the darkness completely, but there is now enough light that I can see again. I can see that maybe God does indeed have a future in mind for me, whether or not that involves romantic love and sex again.

The point is not whether I will or won't or should or shouldn't have sex. The point is the same one I came to at the conclusion of the last chapter: I can't figure this out by myself, and I don't have to. I might be divorced but I am not "single." I have a family. I am part of a Body that holds me up. God has been loving me in the best way possible — through other people. Those people are going to walk with me through whatever comes next.

For the first two years of my divorce, the idea of dating repulsed me. It lost every spark of allure and excitement that I felt in my twenties. All I could think about is that romance leads to marriage, and marriage leads to pain. While a big part of me still thinks that, I am starting to believe in the possibility what psychoanalysts call *corrective emotional experience*. I believe that it might — just maybe — be possible for me to experience something redemptive that restores my faith in love and marriage. So in the past few months, I have been open to the idea of dating. I'm not dating anyone yet and maybe I never will, but I no longer recoil at the thought of venturing through the ups and down of romantic love. We'll see what happens. Regardless, I now know that being single need not ever mean being alone. That's making it easier, if not exactly *easy*, to contemplate the possibility of trying out a new relationship someday.

You are still noticing that I haven't really talked about sex yet, right? You caught me.

I have so many theological and psychological thoughts about sex after divorce. My emotions run the gamut from fear to shame to excitement. I have no idea what is going to happen, but here is what I do know: The love of God and the people God has put in my life will sustain me and repair any mistakes I make, whether those mistakes result from being too cautious or too impulsive. And I will certainly make mistakes. Sexuality is complicated. It's messy. It's something made perfect and whole at creation that sin shattered into a thousand pieces. So it's a good thing God's grace is bigger than all my mistakes. It's a good thing I can work through all this broken mess in relationships with the people in my life.

Above all, divorced people need community. They need family. This is what the Church needs to provide. Divorced people need this far more than platitudes, guidelines, and five-point plans about what to do after divorce. They need people to show them that they are part of the Body of Christ. This means more than just praying for them and greeting them at church. Divorced people undergo not only emotional isolation: Life just becomes harder. Life tasks that were once shared are now left to one person. Something as commonplace as getting a new piece of furniture or transporting children to school can become massive undertakings. Life as a single parent can be overwhelming. Forget finding time to date; finding time to go to the store can be a challenge. Divorced people need multiple layers of support. The unfortunate reality, however, is that divorced Christians often receive just the opposite. The Church has little to no structures in place for them. They have to overcome the assumption, if not outright accusations, that their divorce was the result of spiritual and moral failure. They become more isolated as they "fall short" of the Church's idealization of marriage and family.

We cannot expect divorced people to solve the puzzle of sexuality while ostracized from their faith community. If they feel like they have failed in their faith, they begin to drown in shame. Shame never leads to healthy sexuality and good decisions. Instead, it leads to hopelessness. That hopelessness can, in turn, lead to anything from reckless impulsivity to depressed isolation. Feeling loved, accepted, and supported, however, helps people work through feelings of loss and shame. It restores hope. As long as I rely on God and my community, everything will be okay. Grace and love will light the darkness as I search, once again, for what it means to be a single, sexual follower of Christ.

References

American Psychiatric Association. (2013). *Diagnostic and statistical manual of mental disorders* (5th ed.). Washington, DC: American Psychiatric Association.

Bailey, B. (2004). From "Bundling" to "Hooking Up": Teaching the History of American Courtship. *OAH Magazine of History*, pp. 3–4.

Baumeister, R. F., & Vohs, K. D. (2004). Sexual economics: Sex as female resource for social exchange in heterosexual interactions. *Personality and Social Psychology Review, 8*(4), pp. 339–363.

Bersamin, M. M., Walker, S., Waiters, E. D., Fisher, D. A., & Grube, J. W. (2005). Promising to wait: Virginity pledges and adolescent sexual behavior. *Journal of Adolescent Health, 36*(5), pp. 428–436.

Buber, M. (1958). The I-thou theme, contemporary psychotherapy, and psychodrama. *Pastoral Psychology, 9*(5), pp. 57–58.

Fiorenza, E. S. (1993). *But she said: Feminist practices of biblical interpretation.* Boston, MA: Beacon Press.

Frost, R. (1975). *The road not taken.* Keene, NH: Stemmer House Publishers.

Green, L. C. (2015). Threat of divorce hard to spot in churchgoing couples. Retrieved from http://blog.lifeway.com/newsroom/2015/10/29/threat-of-divorce-hard-to-spot-among-churchgoing-couples/

Meltzer, B. N., Petras, J. W., & Reynolds, L. T. (1975). *Symbolic interactionism: Genesis, varieties and criticism.* New York, NY: Routledge.

Miller, D. (2009). *A million miles in a thousand years: What I learned while editing my life.* Nashville, TN: Thomas Nelson Inc.

Miller, D. (2003). *Blue like jazz: Nonreligious thoughts on spirituality.* Nashville, TN: Thomas Nelson Inc.

Nelson, J. B. (1978). *Embodiment: An approach to sexuality and Christian theology.* Minneapolis, MN: Fortress Press.

Nouwen, H. J. (2016). *The Return of the Prodigal Son* (Anniversary Edition: A Special Two-in-One Volume, including Home Tonight). New York, NY: Convergent Books.

Regnerus, M. (2007). *Forbidden fruit: Sex & religion in the lives of American teenagers.* New York, NY: Oxford University Press.

Shaughnessy, M. F., & Shakesby, P. (1992). Adolescent sexual and emotional intimacy. *Adolescence, 27*(106), p. 475.

Tosches, N. (1991). *Unsung Heroes of Rock 'n' Roll: The Birth of Rock 'n' Roll in the Wild Years Before Elvis*. Three Rivers, MI: Three Rivers Press.

About the Author

Steve Simpson is a psychologist, an author, and a professor in the Graduate School of Psychology at Fuller Theological Seminary. He is the author of *What Women Wish You Knew about Dating* and *Assaulted by Joy,* and co-author of *What Wives Wish Their Husbands Knew about Sex.* He is the father of adolescent quadruplets and who fill his heart with joy while constantly reminding him that he is no longer cool.